The
BATTLE
of the
FIVE SPOT

OTHER BOOKS BY DAVID LEE

Music
Stopping Time: Paul Bley and the Transformation of Jazz
(with Paul Bley)

Literature
Into the Night Life:
Canadian Writers and Artists at Work
(edited with Maureen Cochrane)

Outdoors
Four-Wheeling on Southern Vancouver Island
Chainsaws: A History

The
BATTLE
of the
FIVE SPOT

Ornette Coleman
and the
New York Jazz Field

DAVID LEE

The Mercury Press

The publisher gratefully acknowledges the financial assistance of the Canada Council for the Arts, the Ontario Arts Council, the Ontario Media Development Corporation, and the Ontario Book Publishing Tax Credit Program. The publisher further acknowledges the financial support of the Government of Canada through the Department of Canadian Heritage's Book Publishing Industry Development Program (BPIDP) for our publishing activities.

Canada Council for the Arts   Conseil des Arts du Canada   Canada

Editor: Beverley Daurio
Cover design and composition: Beverley Daurio
Title page photograph of Ornette Coleman © Ray Avery

Printed and bound in Canada
Printed on acid-free paper

1 2 3 4 5   10 09 08 07 06

Library and Archives Canada Cataloguing in Publication

Lee, David, 1952-
The battle of the Five Spot : Ornette Coleman and the New York
jazz field / David Lee.

ISBN 1-55128-123-6
1. Jazz—New York (N.Y.)—History and criticism. 2. Coleman,
Ornette. I. Title.
ML3508.8.N5L477 2006   781.6509747'1   C2006-904323-X

The Mercury Press
Box 672, Station P Toronto, Ontario Canada M5S 2Y4
www.themercurypress.ca

Contents

PREFACE
The Five Spot of Our Dreams

For a few moments in the winter of 1980, Bill Smith and I paused while walking down a cold Manhattan street as Bill pointed out to me a cluttered, abandoned storefront that had once been the Five Spot Café.

By this time, I had spent several years working for Coda Publications, a bustling quasi-collective enterprise run out of a succession of rundown storefronts in downtown Toronto. Founded by English expatriates John Norris (who had started *Coda* magazine in 1958) and Bill Smith, the full scope of its activities included not just the magazine, but a record store and mail order service, the Sackville record label, and concert series in local theatres, clubs and bars.

In the summer of 1975 I was new to Toronto as a recent west-coast émigré, a mediocre acoustic guitarist, and a fan of rock and folk music. Freshly unemployed, I dropped into the Jazz & Blues Centre to spend my last few dollars on a record by an artist I had just discovered, Gil Evans. I ran into one of my neighbours from Gothic Avenue, who worked upstairs on subscriptions and typesetting for the magazine. She and her husband were leaving town, Peggy told me, *Coda* needed a replacement, and did I know anyone who would be interested? When I nominated myself, she showed me around the main floor, its walls graffitied with the signatures of artists from Anthony Braxton to B.B. King, and the office upstairs.

As soon as I installed myself in that environment, hot and muggy as a Toronto summer, filled with traffic noise from Yonge Street and non-stop music from the ever-rotating turntable downstairs, it was no more than a few days, perhaps hours, before I was infected with the love of the music that had already done so much to shape the courses of Bill's and John's lives, and was to do the same for mine.

Soon I set aside my fretted folk instruments and bought a used double bass, and by the time we stopped in front of the old Five Spot, I had been studying and playing bass for several years. A year before, Bill (who played soprano saxophone) and I, searching for a drummer with whom to form a trio, instead had found a violinist, David Prentice. Our basic approach to performance was to organize tightly focused free improvisations around simple written passages, mostly composed by Bill. It was a style of music referred to at the time as "avant-garde jazz," and considering the possibilities for a group of that sort in Canada we were wildly successful. In the next few years we were to tour and record, and collaborate not only with fellow musicians from Canada, the US and overseas, but poets, dancers, playwrights and filmmakers. Playing improvised music was my entry to a luxuriant cultural feast of the imagination in which anything seemed possible.

"Clo and I went there," Bill recalled of the Five Spot, "as soon as we got off the plane. We heard the Charles Mingus Quintet." Twenty years later, there was nothing about the place that recalled its glory days, and after a minute Bill and I moved on. One reason that I remember this brief interlude is that we had just recorded our first LP, "Pick a Number," with David Prentice. With that milestone we felt we might possibly claim a connection to the Five Spot's tradition of musical adventure, not just as fans of the music, but as players.

Although long since closed, the café was still going strong in our imaginations. The original Five Spot was by all accounts an unimpressive place, made legendary by the fabulous talents who performed there—the avant garde of its time. The closest we would ever come to it was in jokes we made on the road, exhausted jazz-lovers fantasizing an afterlife spent in an eternal nightclub with the beer always cold, the grand piano always in tune, and clean restrooms. In this Five Spot of our dreams, paradise would be spent at the bar with Billie Holiday and Bud Powell as they waited to perform, while onstage Charles Mingus played his greatest set, Bird and Eric Dolphy trading fours.

Meanwhile, in this life, I managed to return to the Five Spot in a way I never suspected: as a scholar, decades after those moments on the New York pavement. In writing this book, I was able to revisit my own Five Spot of the mind. Here, especially in the club's most famous episode, Ornette Coleman's New York debut, I was able to research not only the music, but the milieu. As cultural feasts go, there was never anything quite like the Five Spot, the artists and personalities onstage and in the audience. Examining this milieu in terms of culture and power as well as in terms of music, it is not at all my intention to disparage the business of art or dispel the magic that it works. The purpose of art, the purpose of most cultural work, is to discover and reveal ourselves and to understand what makes us tick, as individuals and as social creatures. As I believe Joseph Jarman—another Five Spot artist—once said, to love who we are and what we do, but to never stop questioning ourselves.

David Lee
July 2006

INTRODUCTION
The Field of the Five Spot

The Five Spot Café was a small, unpretentious, even shabby bar at Five Cooper Square in the Bowery, a traditionally working-class neighbourhood in Lower Manhattan. Because of its location east of the clubs, lofts and galleries of Greenwich Village, the Bowery was home to many artists and intellectuals from the village scene, some of whom would gather at the Five Spot.[1]

The club had a piano, which occasionally one of the customers would play, and in 1956 the brothers Joe and Iggy Termini, who had inherited the Five Spot from their father, initiated a jazz policy.[2] They presented such modern artists as Thelonious Monk, Randy Weston and David Amram, as well as the radical young avant-garde pianist Cecil Taylor. Taylor's six-week engagement "immediately attracted a new crowd of artists, writers, and members of what at that time was commonly referred to as the Uptown Bohemia. The skids went out, the sawdust came off the floor, the prices went up," and by the end of the year the Five Spot had become an outpost, pioneering the transformation of its neighbourhood into the East Village—an eastward extension of the long-established Greenwich Village artistic community.[3]

By the time Ornette Coleman premiered there on November 17, 1959, the Five Spot had featured such jazz artists as Herbie Nichols, Charles Mingus and Monk's quartet with John Coltrane.[4] None of these artists were the commercial jazz stars of the era, but all of them were counted among its leading jazz innovators.

Whether or not the Terminis' investment in the jazz avant garde was a function of their own tastes in music, their hiring of these particular musicians was a canny move to make at this particular time and place.[5] After all, the Five Spot's neighbourhood bordered on Greenwich Village in Lower Manhattan, a home and/or business centre for artists, intellectuals, journalists, art dealers and students, and a destination for thousands of visitors from outside the city or abroad, many of whom also had a vested interest in the arts. This neighbourhood's sheer volume of intellectual traffic put the Terminis in a rare position: one in which the presentation of "art for art's sake" in a non-subsidized commercial venue could turn out to be a sound business decision.

Stories from the era concur that the avant-garde jazz musicians at the Five Spot frequently played to full houses.[6] The audience often included "bohemians" from all disciplines: jazz musicians as well as critics and media personalities. The clientele during Coleman's engagement included painters Robert Rauschenberg, Larry Rivers and Franz Kline, writers Norman Mailer and Jack Kerouac, and conductor Leonard Bernstein, as well as the African-American writers James Baldwin and Amiri Baraka (then known as LeRoi Jones).[7]

In making the Five Spot a centre of international controversy, Coleman's premiere completed the transformation of this Lower East Side neighbourhood into the "East Village." The transformation had started in the early 1950s. As rents rose in Greenwich Village and other parts of Manhattan, writers such as Allen Ginsberg, Kerouac and Mailer moved into the neighbourhood. In 1959, writers as diverse as playwright Jack Gelber, poet Frank O'Hara, Baraka and his wife Hettie Jones, and W.H. Auden all lived within a few blocks of the Five Spot.[8] On hearing of the death of Billie Holiday on July 17, 1959, O'Hara wrote a poem ending with the lines:

and I am sweating a lot by now and thinking of
leaning on the john door in the 5 SPOT
while she whispered a song along the keyboard
to Mal Waldron and everyone and I stopped breathing...[9]

According to Edmiston and Cirino's *Literary New York,* Joe and Iggy Termini "let musicians like Billie Holiday perform without cabaret cards, and writers and artists listen without paying."[10] As a supposed counter-inducement to drug abuse, the city of New York withdrew the "cabaret card" from musicians with narcotics offences such as Holiday. In a community ravaged by drugs, it had no effect on their use, but kept many talented musicians from performing while at the height of their powers—including, for example, Thelonious Monk, who was known never to use drugs but who, as a passenger in a car during a police search, had taken the blame for drugs that actually belonged to a friend.

For a writer at the time to mention that the Five Spot was hiring Holiday would only make trouble for everyone, so none of them let the cat out of the bag. However, it may reveal something of the relationship of the Five Spot to its local community. Presumably it would be unwise to use poster and newspaper advertising for an engagement that was technically illegal, but in a neighbourhood such as the East Village, the Five Spot could draw an audience for Holiday simply by word of mouth.

In short, the Five Spot was a very special place. Greenwich Village historian Terry Miller goes to far as to claim of the club that "a new underground formed here, and painters, writers and jazz musicians joined forces to stage an assault on the very definitions of art, music, theater, and literature."[11]

ONE
The Arrival of Ornette Coleman

On November 17, 1959, the Ornette Coleman Quartet began a two-week engagement at the Five Spot Café, bringing with them a radical and controversial new approach to jazz performance. The quartet—Coleman, alto saxophone; Don Cherry, pocket trumpet; Charlie Haden, bass; and Billy Higgins, drums—drew large and engaged audiences:[12]

> [Composer/conductor Leonard] Bernstein pronounced Ornette Coleman a genius. John Coltrane came down to play with him between sets. Lionel Hampton asked to sit in...Thelonious Monk said that what Coleman was doing was "bad"... Charles Mingus was ambivalent... So was Miles Davis... Someone set a car on fire out front; someone else burst into the kitchen between sets and punched Coleman. Most jazz writers were hostile, too.[13]

Coleman's arrival in New York spurred a controversy that in many ways is still active in the music almost fifty years later.[14]

Amazingly, there seem to have been no recordings made of any of Coleman's many Five Spot performances, but his music from the time was documented in many studio dates. In these, we can hear clear differences between Coleman's music and the prevailing styles of the time. The quartet's arrangements consist largely of "heads"—melodies played by the horns in loose unison or with improvised counterpoint over rhythmic accompaniment, that bookend an otherwise improvised performance. The instrumentation is sparse—alto saxophone, trumpet, bass and drums float free of the reassuring harmonic basis—or the regimented tunings—of a chordal instrument such as piano or guitar. The ensemble's intonation is loose and vocalized rather than strict and tempered—a band member plays sharp or flat, with coarse or smooth tones according to his expressive needs, and the others respond accordingly.

Yet usually the music is in a fixed rhythm and it even "swings"—the band plays 4/4 time with classic jazz exuberance, looseness and buoyancy. Many of Coleman's compositions have entered the jazz repertoire;

Lonely Woman quickly became a jazz standard and has remained so for years, and other Coleman compositions have been performed and recorded by countless groups. So it can be hard for the contemporary listener to understand why the quartet's music inspired such vehement objections. Decades after the fact, we tend to look back bemusedly, fondly, even condescendingly, on the furor that surrounded Coleman at the Five Spot. After, all, Coleman's music did *not* turn out to be a trick or a fad. Clearly, it was a logical extension of the jazz that came before it.

Then why did the music cause such an outcry? At the dawn of the twenty-first century, are we somehow smarter and more sophisticated than the movers and shakers in the jazz field were almost fifty years ago? Or were there other currencies circulating besides the principal item tendered throughout the controversy: the ostensible question of whether Coleman's music was "bad" or "good?" The arguments against Coleman that have been passed down to us in jazz histories and textbooks tend to be arguments about technique and aesthetics. But for musicians, critics and scholars, there was much more at stake. Among Coleman's supporters, for example, a central question in evaluating the music was not whether Coleman's approach was any "good"—that was agreed—but whether it was *important*. Was it going to influence jazz as a whole, even become the new mainstream of jazz performance practice? Or would it prove to be a stylistic dead end—a music admired but little imitated, or a music that after the furor of its debut, would simply be forgotten?

The music has by no means been forgotten, but a review of the issues surrounding it—issues just as pressing now as they were in 1959—is overdue. These other issues influenced the reception of Coleman's music just as much as the way the music actually *sounded*.

In the course of researching these issues, I found help from a surprising source when I came across the theory of artistic and intellectual "fields" that has been constructed by the French philosopher and sociologist Pierre Bourdieu (1930–2002). As far as I could tell, Bourdieu's depictions of the role of the avant garde, the movements between "positions and position-takings," and the influence of "consecrating figures" in an artistic field, fit the range of reactions that greeted Coleman's music.

Working from Bourdieu's model, and defining jazz as an artistic field unto itself, we can begin to perceive within the literature of the jazz world—interviews, journalism, criticism, advertisements, liner notes and scholarly essays—the currents of power, the webs of influence, the flux of positions and position-takings that Bourdieu sees as characteristic of a field. Within a field, for example, the avant garde has a very special role, and we can see how precisely and dramatically Ornette Coleman stepped into this role when he made his first recordings, and then debuted his quartet's music in New York City.

Welcomed by some, resisted by others, Coleman's seemingly sudden arrival in New York in 1959 was unexpected, radical and disturbing. It revealed the work of the field's incumbents in a new light; then one by one and in varying degrees, it displaced them. In general, those who had aligned themselves with "the shape of jazz to come" by championing Coleman were happy with their revised roles. From others, relegated overnight from the music's advance guard to its worthy but less remarkable rank and file, there were howls of outrage.

The positions of field members at the time are well-documented. Perhaps because the controversy around Coleman was so intense, it seems that few of the field's members chose (or were allowed by the quote-hungry media) to be passive listeners, or to distance themselves from the debate. From accounts of tensions and showdowns in the Five Spot itself, to newspaper articles, interviews, critical essays and *Down Beat* blindfold tests, at one time or another representatives of all positions within the field had to declare themselves in relation to Coleman. In declaring themselves, each revealed his or her position, for better or worse.

Considering the cultural disparity between Bourdieu's areas of study and American jazz, it is not surprising that his ideas do not always fit perfectly around the figures who shaped jazz music. A twentieth-century jazz club is not a nineteenth-century Parisian *salon*. What is surprising is how often they *can* be seen to make that fit.

Descriptions of the Five Spot at the time of Coleman's debut embody Bourdieu's concept of the field made real, as a dank, crowded Lower Manhattan tavern. Onstage are the avant-garde artists, fresh from

California, excited about their music but uncertain of its reception. At the bar we find the New York musicians, black and white, watching each others' reactions, attentive to the music, but also attentive to the new light it shines upon their own work, in artistic and in professional terms. Behind the bar are the owners, pleased that this programming gamble has paid off, their livelihoods and those of their staff depending on the balance they can maintain between sponsoring "art for art's sake" and selling as many drinks as possible to each customer. And in the audience the New York intelligentsia, some with a professional stake in the jazz field, some with the passion of dedicated amateurs. Others are there because they simply know that this is the important place to be; drinking, listening, declaiming, flirting, networking and arguing for or against the music and its future. The arena of the Five Spot Café was an artistic field shorn of all abstractions, in which the sound of the music, the judgements of the critics, and the personal tastes of each of its members became essential currencies in determining each member's professional status and position.

When Coleman arrived in New York, his music had to run the gauntlet of the city's jazz field, to weather the dynamics, the politics and the power structures of a community that had sustained several generations and numerous styles of jazz creativity. How his music fared in that milieu determined its reception by members of the national and international jazz field: musicians, critics, jazz listeners, and the readership of the countless newspapers and magazines that reported on this new way of playing the music. This book explores, among other things, the interpretation of Coleman's music in terms of Bourdieu's thought, to see if it might lead to a fuller understanding of how the music was heard at the time, and a clearer picture of its relationship to contemporaneous music and musicians.

Hopefully this experiment will work both ways. *The Battle of the Five Spot* also tries to test the validity of Bourdieu's theories against the concrete examples provided by accounts of Coleman's performances at the Five Spot, by reviews of his first recordings, and by other documentation of the jazz community of the time.

I hope to illustrate how the music's initial reception in 1959 continues to affect our perception of it now, and to help clarify how and why Coleman's music, and the man himself, have been assigned such unique positions in the canons of jazz history.

TWO
Jazz and Ornette Coleman

At the time of Coleman's New York debut, jazz was well-established as a music based on a variety of song forms, primarily the blues and the popular song as defined by Broadway musicals and Tin Pan Alley song-writers. The music had a documented history with a widely accepted canon of major figures, many of whom were still alive and performing. Yet it was, as it remains today, a genre subject to a variety of social and musical tensions.[15]

BLACK ART, WHITE HEGEMONY

The greatest of these tensions was racial. Few have ever disputed that jazz was originated by black Americans who brought unique and original approaches to a variety of European-based song forms. But like African-Americans themselves, the music faced ongoing problems of identity and representation within a white hegemony in which European musical traditions still carried the greatest cultural currency.[16] These problems were made worse by the speed with which white musicians appropriated new approaches and new techniques as quickly as black musicians could introduce them. This was true in 1917 with the Original Dixieland Jazz Band, in the 1920s with Paul Whiteman, in the 1930s with Benny Goodman and in the 1940s with Woody Herman— in every case white artists won popular success by presenting styles, compositions and arrangements that originated with black artists who were themselves chronically marginalized by the music industry.

The first jazz record was made in 1917 by the Original Dixieland Jazz Band, a white group that had thoroughly assimilated the style of black New Orleans jazz.[17] The record became a hit, and set the pattern within the music industry for white musicians appropriating black styles, promoting them as "jazz" and claiming the lion's share of the work's potential for commercial profit.[18] It was six years until a black group (under the leadership of Joe "King" Oliver) made a similar break-through.[19]

During the 1920s, despite the remarkable music being made by black artists such as Fletcher Henderson and Duke Ellington, it was the white bandleader Paul Whiteman who successfully promoted himself as "the King of Jazz"—even though what his orchestra played at tea dances and ballrooms was "society" music influenced by jazz rather than what we today consider jazz. At a milestone 1924 concert, Whiteman premiered George Gershwin's *Rhapsody in Blue*, a historic synthesis of jazz influences and classical instrumentation—and, one must regretfully point out, a milestone in paying obeisance to the beauties of black American music, without actually employing a single black performer, arranger or composer. In 1930 Whiteman starred in an early sound film which confirmed him eponymously as *The King of Jazz*, during an era which saw relatively modest gains made by innovative, influential, and often popular black artists such as Duke Ellington, Louis Armstrong and Fletcher Henderson.[20]

In the 1930s, despite the prominence of the early swing groups led by Fats Waller, Luis Russell, and Count Basie, the white clarinetist Benny Goodman became hugely popular, buoyed by the growing powers of radio and the record industry and often using arrangements purchased from Fletcher Henderson, Benny Carter and other black musicians who did not have Goodman's performance and recording opportunities.[21] Carter, for example, went to Europe to find work during the 1930s (as did the music's premier tenor saxophonist, Coleman Hawkins). Henderson, whose arranging techniques were a major influence on the big-band style that dominated the Swing Era, is today better-known to the jazz scholar than to the general listener.[22] The music industry's marginalization of his hugely influential and highly accessible music was so notorious that decades after his death, CBS subtitled a four-album reissue of his music *A Study in Frustration*.[23]

Similarly in the 1950s, many black jazz artists felt eclipsed by the publicity and popularity garnered by pianist Dave Brubeck—featured on the cover of *Time* magazine, yet considered by aficionados to be inferior to most of his black contemporaries.[24] To this day, this cultural disjunct continues. If we think of the music industry as a record store, in one window it celebrates and displays jazz as the great African-American art form, and in the next window it promotes the latest white jazz star. Even today in this virtual record store, when Wynton Marsalis and others are actively trying to reclaim jazz culturally as an African-American art form, they would find themselves sharing an industry window along with reissues of recordings by Miles Davis, Thelonious Monk, Billie Holiday, Duke Ellington and Louis Armstrong. The neighbouring window would be wholly given over to the era's most heavily marketed jazz artist, the blonde Canadian singer/pianist, Diana Krall.

JAZZ AS HIGH ART

Another major tension was caused by the uncertain status of jazz within the popular music industry. Art or entertainment? Even before 1920, the Swiss conductor Ernest Ansermet[25] and the American critic Olin Downes[26] had written that certain aspects of jazz music deserved serious critical attention; they are the first writers on record to treat jazz as high art, rather than discounting it as a trivial entertainment catering only to popular tastes. Gradually over the years, other voices joined theirs in urging that the music could, and should, be listened to seriously and with discernment.

However, the declarations of critics that jazz was indeed a "high art" carried no weight in the milieux where the musicians actually earned their livelihoods. The music was still played in venues where it needed to turn a profit, in ticket sales or bar receipts or both. The sophisticated vocal and instrumental techniques, original concepts and emotional expressiveness so praised by critics had to be conveyed in a form that would not distract an audience that had paid to drink, dance and socialize.

As the century progressed, jazz music's relatively low status as a serious performing art was increasingly (if rarely effectively) protested by determined musicians, critics and scholars. If anything, the music's artistic status was raised somewhat during the 1940s by three factors: the positions taken by leading bebop figures such as Dizzy Gillespie, the advance into concert halls made by musicians such as Duke Ellington and Benny Goodman and promoters such as Norman Granz, and the music's waning power as the mainstream of popular style (which made "high art" status more appealing to musicians who saw it as the best of their dwindling options).

Within the jazz field, musicians who tried to present their work as high art often found themselves selling a product for which the market was meagre and unpredictable. Although jazz players were making slow incursions into the subsidized "art" markets of college and university performances and "legitimate" concert series, by and large their livelihoods depended on their abilities to attract paying customers to jazz clubs. However despite their best efforts, by the 1950s many of those customers were being lost to rhythm-and-blues and the rising tide of rock-and-roll.

By the time Coleman came to the Five Spot, jazz had managed to achieve at least an entry-level status as a "high art" within the field of Western music. Jazz was presented in colleges and universities and occasionally in concert series alongside classical and folk music. In 1957 a summer program, the Lenox School of Jazz in Massachusetts, was established as an academic proving-grounds for the teaching of jazz history, composition and performance.

But these modest advances into a field traditionally dominated by European classical music were by no means welcomed by all the members of that field. Although enthusiastically endorsed, analyzed and studied by a host of intellectuals, bohemians and educated listeners, jazz had been allowed only as far as the margins of the classical hegemony, without actually being ushered inside. There were, after all, no cultural mediators more vigilant than those who guarded the gates of the classical music world. Anyone who did not readily fit the traditional model of the European artiste had difficulty gaining admission, regardless of their abilities (in fact, the insularity of the classical world helps to identify it clearly as a legitimate cultural "field," as we will see when we get to Pierre Bourdieu). By definition this excluded African-American artists, but it also extended to jazz styles of composing, arranging and improvising.

JAZZ AND THE SONG FORM

Through all these conflicts of identity, there were two constants in the history of jazz. One was improvisation, which had been essential to the music since its earliest days (and which was to be offered bountifully by the Coleman quartet). The other was the association of jazz music with the song form, a constant which Coleman, alarmingly, seemed to be in the process of discarding.

By the time that Coleman appeared on the scene, jazz had proven in nightly performances, and had documented in forty years of recordings, that the song form, although outwardly constricting, could be constantly reinvented through new approaches to arrangement and interpretation. Above all, the song form was the essential context for the improvisations that were considered by many to be jazz music's defining feature. The art of the jazz improviser was the art of improvising over the "changes"—the chord sequences of popular songs.

Jazz musicians were constantly testing the limits of the song form: investigating and instigating new procedures, new approaches to harmony, new relationships between soloists and accompanists in small and large ensembles. To date, the jazz canon of seminal composers and improvisers had worked exclusively, if not within the song form itself, then within the chord changes that were its signature method of harmonic progression. Tenor saxophonist Coleman Hawkins, trumpeter Louis Armstrong, clarinetist Benny Goodman and singer Ella Fitzgerald, for example, were all established virtuosos, capable of extended improvisations which stretched the harmonic boundaries of the song's chord progressions, but departed from them only for special effect. The same was true of the "bebop" generation who came to prominence in the 1940s and 1950s; although the new melodies they composed to the chord changes of jazz standards were more intricate and presented daunting technical challenges, their dependence on the song form was just as implicit.

Early in 1959, trumpeter Miles Davis' album "Kind of Blue" had introduced "modal" playing to jazz. Although these compositions were built on harmonically simpler structures, they effectively maintained the familiar pattern of sequencing chord changes for the duration of a performance.

The song form remained the basis of the jazz canon, a canon adjudicated by enthusiastic listeners, critics and record collectors, disseminated by radio broadcasts, live performances and recordings, and maintained by records, published editions, "fake sheets" and transcriptions.

JAZZ IN THE 1950S

In the mid-1950s, musicians such as Art Blakey and Horace Silver developed a style of small-group jazz that was melodically and rhythmically simpler and more overtly blues-based than the prevailing bebop styles. What came to be known as "hard bop" was more accessible and danceable than bebop. At its best, as in Silver's and Blakey's groundbreaking groups, it was tightly arranged and immaculately presented, featuring inventive soloists improvising tunefully and virtuosically over bluesy chord changes.

Hard bop could be seen as a populist reaction to bebop—the attempt to reaffirm jazz as a popular music. In the gospel-influenced voicings often favoured by its composers (Silver, Lee Morgan, Bobby Timmons), in its leanings towards the blues rather than the popular song, and in the fact that most of its proponents were black, it has also been seen as reaffirmation of traditional African-American musical values, in the face of perceived attempts to align jazz with the Western classical tradition.[27]

In fact, just such attempts constituted another of the era's major movements in jazz. Beginning in the late 1940s with the work of instrumentalist/composers such as Miles Davis, Gil Evans, Gerry Mulligan and Gunther Schuller, this movement was seen, in Schuller's words, as a "confluence of two idioms [which may] broaden into a self-sufficient third stream."[28] Within this "Third Stream," jazz composers experimented with new forms, and improvisers accordingly strove to find new ways to improvise within these forms. Although Third Stream never became a sufficiently widespread practice to become a "mainstream" of its own, before Coleman's debut it was widely regarded as an inevitable step in the evolution of jazz. As Schuller wrote, some months before Ornette Coleman came to New York, jazz and classical music "have been veering toward each other for some forty years, and have, in recent years, become tangent."[29]

Cool jazz was poised between the very different areas covered by hard bop and the third stream movement, and indeed "poised" could be taken as an apt description of the music itself. Although an often-passionate style, its tendency was towards slower tempos, tighter and more controlled instrumental timbres, and, in especial contrast to the improvisational fireworks of bebop, an overall feeling if not of relaxation, then of effortlessness in its soloists.

The Miles Davis Nonet sessions of 1949–50 have been issued on record as "The Birth of the Cool," not at all inaccurately since they more or less coincide with the beginnings of the style and display in concentrated form its most salient characteristics of skilled contrapuntal arrangements and "cool" soloing. Musicians classified within the "cool" school actually include a range of styles: The Modern Jazz Quartet, Dave Brubeck's quartet with Paul Desmond, Gerry Mulligan's quartets (especially those with Chet Baker) and Jimmy Giuffre. Miles Davis in his person and in his music was simultaneously the epitome of the "cool" musician, and a wide-ranging artist whose works span all three of these categories. Between "The Birth of the Cool" and his 1959 "Sketches of Spain" collaboration with Gil Evans, his outstanding work in the hard bop, "cool" and Third Stream genres underscores the intensity he brought to all of his projects, and perhaps also the highly permeable quality of these musical categories.

THREE
Ornette Coleman in Los Angeles

Ornette Coleman began playing the alto saxophone in his early teens. Unable to afford a teacher, he taught himself by reading instruction books and learning songs from the radio. Although he enthusiastically experimented with the instrument's potential—"I used to play one note all day, and I used to try to find how many different sounds I could get out of the mouthpiece"—he lacked a mentor to mediate and clarify his studies, and formed concepts about the facts of scales and transpositions that were, to say the least, highly idiosyncratic.[30] Years later, Gunther Schuller, after befriending Coleman in New York, giving him private theory lessons, and transcribing a number of his compositions, concluded that Coleman—

> studied (on his own) harmony and theory textbooks, and gradually evolved a radically new concept and style, seemingly from a combination of musical intuition, born of South-western country blues and folk forms, and his misreadings—or highly personal interpretations—of the theoretical texts.[31]

In editing ten of Coleman's pieces to be published by MJQ Music in 1961, Schuller found huge disparities between how the composer notated his pieces, and how he played them. Schuller admitted in the foreword to the edition that he had resorted to transcribing the music from recordings, and flatly declared "Mr. Coleman never learned to read or write conventional musical notation correctly." Schuller continued:

> Lest this be construed as criticism of his abilities, we wish to assure the reader that, were this the case, this publication would never have been undertaken. On the contrary, we believe it is precisely because Mr. Coleman was not "handicapped" by conventional music education that he has been able to make his unique contribution to contemporary music.[32]

Unconventional as it may have been, Coleman's background included intense practising, playing and composing, and personal collaborations, both with jazz-loving peers at I.M. Terrell High School in Fort Worth, and with the more experienced musicians in the working bands where he soon found a professional niche.[33] As his musical compatriot John Carter pointed out:

> [In the mid-1940s] a good many young men who would have been out there playing were in the service. High-school-age boys could go out and get work at what would ordinarily be a man's job—that was true in every area of society, and it was true in music."[34]

As a result, after Coleman's initial self-studies, he spent his mid-to-late teens in an extended apprenticeship, playing for hours every night in blues, rhythm-and-blues and pop bands, touring with a minstrel show, and taking occasional excursions into bebop. A 1950 tour with the blues singer-guitarist Pee Wee Crayton stranded Coleman in Los Angeles. Although he spent part of 1952 and 1953 back in Fort Worth, Los Angeles became Coleman's home until his move east to New York City in 1959.[35]

In Los Angeles, despite the daily challenges he faced simply in order to earn a living, Coleman studied, practised, and eventually evolved his own system of composing and improvising music, a system that he named "harmolodics."[36] As Ian Carr describes harmolodics:

> Each instrument in an ensemble is both a melody and a rhythm instrument; players abandon their traditional roles and instruments which normally accompany share as lead voices in creating the music... Harmonic consonance and resolution become irrelevant, the emphasis being on creating interacting lines.[37]

Coleman expanded and formalized his theory of harmolodics while writing through-composed music for larger ensembles in the 1960s, but he did not use the term in public until the early seventies. When he began leading his own groups in the late 1950s, harmolodics was more clearly manifest in the character of ensemble improvisations, in the way that the bassist and percussionist were encouraged to depart from a composition's structures in order to improvise melodies and counter-rhythms on an equal basis with the horns.

It was this deconstruction of the traditional hierarchy of the small jazz group that perhaps constituted Coleman's greatest influence on the "free jazz" that was to follow him. At its most basic, harmolodics can be interpreted simply as playing by ear, along with a reshuffling of performance priorities and a de-emphasis of the customary roles played by each instrument. In conventional terms this might be (and often has been) interpreted as a relaxation, even an utter abandonment, of musical discipline. However, since early in his career Coleman made clear that his version of musical freedom seeks not to refute traditional musical disciplines, but if anything to liberate them by realizing their fullest implications.

Coleman steadily developed his ideas throughout the 1950s, but had a hard time getting them across. In Los Angeles, he politely followed the protocols of asking to sit in with local and visiting bands, but he was continually ejected from bandstands, or left alone to play by himself, by such musicians as Dexter Gordon, Clifford Brown, Max Roach and Eric Dolphy.[38] However, other local musicians such as Hampton Hawes, Teddy Edwards and Bill Holman encouraged him, and eventually Coleman accumulated a nucleus of colleagues and collaborators who were interested in what he was doing: saxophonist James Clay, trumpeters Bobby Bradford and Don Cherry, drummers Billy Higgins and Ed Blackwell, pianists George Newman, Walter Norris and Don Friedman, and bassists Charlie Haden, Ben Tucker and Don Payne.[39]

It was at Payne's house in 1958 that the Los Angeles bassist Red Mitchell heard Coleman and recommended him to Lester Koenig, the owner of the Contemporary jazz record label. The resulting LP, "Something Else!" brought Coleman a small amount of critical attention, but no offers of work. There was nothing in the wind to suggest that, in a year's time, he would be onstage at the Five Spot, or that his presence in that modest venue would make it the jazz community's centre of attention, but in fact the chain of events that would take him there was already in motion.

TOWARDS ATONALITY IN JAZZ

The Montreal pianist Paul Bley (1932–) attended the Juilliard School of Music from 1949 to 1952 and moved to New York City in 1954. Bley was a musical prodigy who had led his own bands since his early teens. Conservatory-trained, experienced in playing bebop and earlier styles of jazz, he was always on the lookout for new artistic challenges. As such, he was well-situated to grasp the motives behind Coleman's music, and its implications for jazz as a whole.

At the beginning of the 1950s, Juilliard was a centre of Third Stream activity. Although open to innovation, and a pioneer in adding jazz instruction to its curriculum, the school's implicit orientation encouraged its students to envision jazz innovations within the context of the classical tradition. In Bley's words:

> We learned something about the evolution of classical music, which had gone through a parallel sequence of development seventy-five years earlier than jazz. Once you realized that, you could look at the history of this European art music to see what was coming next in jazz. It was easy in 1950 to see that the music was about to become very impressionistic, and so it did... After impressionism, atonality was next. The big mystery wasn't whether atonal music was coming; it was why it wasn't already here. European music had been atonal since the twenties—what was taking jazz so long?[40]

The great barrier between jazz and atonality, Bley maintains, was the influence of alto saxophonist Charlie Parker (nicknamed "Bird," 1920–1955). Parker's innovations in harmony and phrasing had been considerable, but it was his sheer virtuosity on the saxophone that set the standard for jazz instrumentalists in the 1950s. Parker's level of ability inspired younger musicians, but also often frustrated and defeated them.

It was easy to fall into the trap of believing that to progress beyond the Parker style, one must first match his speed of execution. Failing to do that, many musicians overlooked chances to explore the music's other implications. As a result, for approximately a decade from the late 1940s onward, jazz styles evolved around Parker's style rather than beyond it.

A style of music such as bebop implies a consensual manner of playing, and the proper development of a new style assumes mastery of the prevailing style that preceded it. However, few could master their instruments to the extent that Parker mastered his; even if they could copy his tone and phrasing, they could not match the sheer velocity of his playing. Undaunted, many evolving jazz players spent years trying to do exactly that, feeling that the standard set by Parker was a hurdle that must be surmounted if they were to develop their music beyond the boundaries of bebop. As Bley says:

> Bird was more triadic than we like to remember. He placed a great emphasis on the flatted fifth and the raised ninth, and these intervals sounded so dissonant at the time that it seemed that Bird's playing might be a major signpost on the road to atonality...
>
> But here we were in New York trying to force jazz into atonality. It was a concern shared by all of the orchestral writers... If there had been, for example, an alto saxophonist in any of their bands who could equal what they were trying to do, that saxophonist would have become the man of the hour. But the ideas stayed in the score, because as soon as the alto saxophone player stood up to solo, it was Bird again, and didn't refer to any of the advances that were being made in the writing.[41]

The more populist tendencies of hard bop, the "art music" experiments of Third Stream, and the tempered bebop style of cool jazz were all attempts to forge a jazz identity that could move outside of the influence of Charlie Parker. The idea of a technical "advance" beyond bebop seemed impossibly difficult—the necessary development of jazz, onward and upward, was stalled behind a barrier of technique. The African-American composer George Russell depicted the immediate future of jazz as a battlefield in which the composer and the improviser would have to arrive at a *détente* in order to merge their forces against the daunting challenge of moving beyond bebop: "The jazz music of the future... the techniques are going to get more complex... [it] represents a continuance of man's struggle with nature to accept ever-more complex materials and subdue them."[42]

Bley's account of these developments is of special interest, as he was the first among his New York peers to encounter Ornette Coleman's music and to appreciate the alternatives it offered to the stalemate of post-bebop jazz. As a conservatory-trained musician, as a "bebop" pianist who opened his mind to the Coleman experience, and as an analytical and articulate exponent of what Bourdieu might have called the "theory of practice," Bley provides valuable insights into the impact that Coleman had on the jazz field of the time. Once moving to New York, Bley had played with, and learned from, swing veterans such as Lester Young, bebop revolutionaries such as Parker and young modernists such as Charles Mingus and Sonny Rollins. In 1956, a cross-country tour leading his own trio brought him to Los Angeles, where for a time he experimented in free improvisation with a fellow Canadian expatriate, trumpeter Herbie Spanier.

Eventually Bley settled into an extended engagement at the Hillcrest Club, on Washington Boulevard in a largely African-American section of Los Angeles. His quartet consisted of vibraphonist Dave Pike, bassist Charlie Haden and drummer Billy Higgins. One night at the Hillcrest in the autumn of 1958, Higgins invited two of his friends down to the club to sit in with the group. The friends were Ornette Coleman and Don Cherry. To Bley, the resulting music was an epiphany:

> In none of [jazz's prevailing] genres was the music coming together the way that I felt it could. I was mastering all the parts of the music—they were no problem. The problem was defining an approach that would bring them all together—tempo and non-tempo, atonality and tonality, written and improvised—in a new and profound way... As hard as Herbie and I worked to put all these elements together, and as hard as the Third Stream composers were

trying to put it together, we were all waiting for something, we knew not what. Unknown to us, we were waiting for Ornette Coleman to join our band at the Hillcrest Club.[43]

By the time he and Cherry sat in at the Hillcrest, Coleman had a large repertoire of his own compositions. Upon hearing them, Bley fired his vibraphonist, hired the two young horn players, and set about learning this new music. This was an unusual way for a professional jazz musician, experienced in the song form, to greet the new approach that Coleman and Cherry brought to the bandstand. When Coleman moved to New York, most of Bley's peers in the jazz field did not share his excitement with this new music:

But the real surprise was, when we played a second piece, which was a Coleman original, although the solos started in the key of the original, rather than following an AABA form, they followed an A to Z form. This I had never heard done before by anyone, not by any of the composers who we had hoped would lead us out of the bebop wilderness, and certainly not in front of a rhythm section that was playing time. In a single gesture, all the constraints of repetitive structure fell away.[44]

Coleman's compositions were scored with chord changes marked in the traditional jazz fashion, but during improvisations, soloists frequently departed from the chord changes—and more unusually, so did the bassist, who (once Coleman began leading his own groups) provided the sole harmonic accompaniment.

Upon hearing Coleman's first recordings and experiencing him live at the Five Spot, George Russell became one of his supporters, explaining the music in this way:

Chords have always helped the jazz player to shape melody, maybe to an extent that he is now over-dependent on the chord. Ornette seems to depend mostly on the overall tonality of the song as a point of departure for melody. By this I don't mean the key the music might be in. His pieces don't readily infer key. They could almost be in any key or no key. I mean that the melody and the chords of his compositions have an overall sound which Ornette seems to use as a point of departure. This approach liberates the improviser to sing his own song really, without having to meet the deadline of any particular chord.[45]

The group at the Five Spot—Coleman alto saxophone, Don Cherry trumpet, Charlie Haden bass, Billy Higgins drums—would play 32-bar tunes more or less in the accepted way, but the solo sections would not be in 32-bar increments. In fact, once the melody was played as a "head" arrangement against the prescribed chords, it seemed as if literally anything could happen (Bley's description of an "A to Z" structure)—the musicians were free to play whatever they chose until Coleman cued the end of the piece by playing the "head" again.

It was an approach that overturned standard jazz performance practice. The quartet's music endured a barrage of criticism from musicians, critics, scholars and listeners. It also won loyal supporters within all those categories, but at the time it was difficult to predict who would support Coleman and who would condemn him. The debate over Coleman became a pivotal moment in jazz history, forcing interested parties to reexamine and assert their musical and philosophical positions—in short, to question their own artistic tastes.

FOUR
Beauty Is a Rare Thing

Despite the lack of recordings of Coleman's many Five Spot performances from autumn 1959 to spring 1960, a quartet version of Coleman's
Beauty Is a Rare Thing, a studio recording made the following July with
Ed Blackwell instead of Higgins on drums, embodies some of the musical traits that elicited such powerful and mixed reactions.

Beauty Is a Rare Thing is, after *Lonely Woman*, probably the Coleman
composition most played by other musicians, usually in a slow "ballad"
style. Coleman opens this version, playing the melody through twice
with rubato (i.e. not in a strict rhythm); Blackwell responding lightly
with mallets, Haden playing arco (bowed) bass as he does throughout.
Cherry's trumpet enters for a short improvised passage before the
melody is played again.

After the melody is played a third time, there ensues a group
improvisation that is like nothing previously recorded in jazz. Haden
introduces a passage of unvarying tremolo ground bass, on strings damp-
ened so that the tonal centre is unclear. Cherry improvises freely over
this background, and Blackwell's percussion, instead of pairing with
Haden in the conventional rhythm section alliance of bass and drums,
focuses instead on Cherry, melodic drum figures in dynamic dialogue
with the trumpet lines. When Coleman enters, playing in the altissimo
register of the alto saxophone, the quartet engages in a brief passage of
improvisation that is rhythmically and harmonically unrelated to anything that has gone before. It does, however, serve the *feeling* of the piece.
Moreover, it confers and confirms the responsibility for developing that
feeling onto the musicians, as improvisers reacting to each other in real
time, rather than as interpreters basing their work upon the original
theme. Although at different times the horns or the bass may play frag-
ments that recall the melody of *Beauty Is a Rare Thing*, the improvisation
is not in the F minor key of the original melody.

The concept behind the piece itself departs radically from what was
then thought of as the jazz tradition, even from the bulk of Coleman's

own recorded repertoire up to this time. At no point are chords implied in the bassist's accompaniment. Instead, Haden plays counterpoint against the melody, as does Cherry in his freewheeling contributions when the melody is reprised at the end of the piece. The improvised nature of the counterpoint is confirmed when the performance ends not on a conventional chord but on a C and G played by the trumpet and saxophone respectively, sustained over an F in the bass.[46]

There is no steady tempo throughout the piece. Although by the late 1950s it was an established practice for the beginning or ending of a jazz piece to be played rubato, the resulting tension—when will steady time return?—was traditionally resolved at some point within the performance by stating the melody in a reassuring fixed tempo. There is no such resolution in *Beauty Is a Rare Thing*. The rubato feeling of the opening melody seems to imply that it is being played against a slow 4/4, but such implications are dispensed with in the improvisations, where the rhythms of the different players—listening and reacting to each other instantly and intuitively—call, respond, and merge with each other into a collective freedom.[47]

Coleman's biographer, John Litweiler, writing in 1992, called this performance "a prophetic work, a usually unacknowledged precedent to the exploration to come among younger New York and especially Chicago jazz artists in the later 1960s."[48] To which one might add the decade's parallel developments of the atonal "non-idiomatic free improvisation" associated with the Spontaneous Music Ensemble in London, the ICP (Instant Composers Pool) in Amsterdam and the musicians recorded by FMP (Free Music Production) in Berlin. In fact, the placement of Coleman's music at the peak of the jazz avant garde was taken by thousands of musicians, all over the world, as permission to explore music through improvisation. Suddenly playing jazz need have nothing to do with the song form—in fact, if improvisation was, as many insisted, the essence of jazz, then it logically followed that to retain the song form—or in some cases, any kind of prearranged structure—could only be an impediment to self-expression.

FIVE

Pierre Bourdieu and the Concept of "Field"

Outside of being born in the same year, Ornette Coleman and Pierre Bourdieu had little in common. Bourdieu (1930–2002), the son of a postman in the French Pyrenees, was an outstanding student who graduated in philosophy from the prestigious Lycée Louis-le-Grand in Paris.[49]

Coleman, an African-American born in Fort Worth, Texas, came from more modest circumstances.[50] His father Randolph was a cook and construction worker who died when Ornette was seven, and his mother Rosa worked as a clerk in a funeral home, as a seamstress and at some point, according to Ornette, "did something like selling Avon products…"[51] When Coleman finished high school, rather than continuing his formal education, he received on-the-job training as a professional musician, playing tenor saxophone in rhythm-and-blues bands to support himself and his mother.

Throughout his twenties, Pierre Bourdieu was always comfortably installed at one institution or another—whether at the *Lycée*, Algiers University, or the Sorbonne. Even as a conscript in the French Army, if Bourdieu missed creature comforts or the company of intellectual peers, he at least knew where his next meal was coming from. During those same years, Ornette Coleman endured the stress and hardships of sporadic and low-paying work as a touring musician, and worked at day jobs as an elevator operator, houseboy and porter.

However, each of them—Bourdieu the sociologist and Coleman the musician—was able to turn his back on the prevailing wisdom of his respective discipline in order to re-interpret that discipline in unique, even radical new ways. Bourdieu claimed of himself that, if he arrived in Algeria in 1955 a philosopher, by the time he left in 1960 he had become a sociologist.[52] It could similarly be said that if, in 1955, Coleman was a struggling jazz saxophonist, by 1960 he was a headline-making musical figure and a recognized jazz innovator.[53] In many ways—certainly in terms of his public profile—the Five Spot Café, during Coleman's residencies in autumn 1959 and spring 1960, was the site of this transformation.

Bourdieu, with his concern for "a theory of practice," was as much sociologist and anthropologist as philosopher. However, during years of applying sociological questions to sociological subjects, he became increasingly self-reflexive, and began to steer his research towards an inquiry of the historical forces that determined just why, at his specific place and time in history, these particular questions should be raised.[54] His writings cover many topics, from the culture of traditional ethnic groups in North Africa to the effect of television in the modern West, but this book refers most heavily to what Jeremy Lane calls Bourdieu's "concept of the 'intellectual field,' that structured space of competing, often antagonistic positions, 'the space of theoretical and methodological possibles,' within which all intellectuals necessarily take a position whenever they speak or write on a particular issue."[55]

Perhaps unusually so for a French intellectual, Bourdieu did not seem greatly interested in jazz.[56] In relating different tastes to different types of art, Bourdieu identifies jazz accurately enough as an art form, along with cinema, comic strips and popular songs, "still in the process of legitimation"—not yet ranked with poetry and classical music in the hierarchy of the high arts, but well on their way. But he does not seem to have been drawn to the music for aesthetic pleasure or for the depths of meaning he found, for example, in nineteenth-century French literature.[57]

Bourdieu's theories were formulated from disparate sources. In Algeria in the 1950s he studied local cultures, observing its citizens both as indigenous peoples pursuing their "traditional" lifestyles and as the subjects of a colonial power. Later, he turned to studies of nineteenth-century French literature, especially the novels of Gustave Flaubert and the intellectual circles in which Flaubert lived and worked.

Unless one is familiar with Algerian ethnology, or French literature, one might find Bourdieu's concept of "field" difficult to grasp for lack of a familiar example—preferably some kind of narrative in which we might see the dynamics of the field enacted. The field whose members came together at the Five Spot provides just such an example. The unwritten criteria for admission to the field, the positions and position-takings, the "consecrating figures" whose decisions can boost or barricade a musical innovator's career—these are all factors that Bourdieu describes in literature and the other arts, and these are all factors that can be seen at work in jazz music during this critical period in its history.

The "jazz world" (and it is very much a world unto itself; Bourdieu goes so far as to call a field a "self-contained universe") includes creators, consumers and mediators: those who make the sounds we call "music," their audience, and the many intermediaries in the music business that connect them. The notion that this world fits Bourdieu's definition of an artistic field is furthered by readings of the author's other works, especially the essays that were first collected in English in the 1993 book *The Field of Cultural Production*, in which he thoroughly defines the idea of the artistic "field."

Bourdieu establishes the importance of position and of "position-taking" within a field, and describes the delicate relationships between a field's members: an intricate ecology in which each individual's movements within the field hierarchy are constantly monitored by the other members. This constant scrutiny is an essential part of the field's structure, because each person's change in status, up or down through the ranks, has the potential to displace the position of any one or all of the field's members. Hence, an artistic or intellectual field is also a field of tensions regarding the maintenance or improvement of its members' positions. The ultimate discretion is applied to the admission or exclusion of new members, who might potentially disrupt the field's status quo.

TASTE

Habitus is the name that Bourdieu gives to the collection of mental structures through which each individual processes incoming information. As Randal Johnson explains it, "the *habitus* is the result of a long process of inculcation, beginning in early childhood, which becomes a 'second sense' or a second nature."[58] It is the individual's *habitus* that assesses new information, applying value judgements that are largely imprinted by the social conditions of his or her upbringing, and delimits the range of practices appropriate for a response. *Habitus* is the reason that a working-class man raised in a household with marginal literacy, and a middle-class man from a highly literate, "cultured" household, can react quite differently when confronting the same problem. Their assessments of the problem and the range of responses each deems appropriate will be shaped by each person's individual *habitus*.[59]

In his 1979 book *Distinction: A Social Critique of the Judgement of Taste,* Bourdieu defines "taste" as a central signifier of social power. As an example, he cites the difference between working-class tastes and the tastes of intellectuals:

> In fact, through the economic and social conditions which [aesthetic judgements] presuppose, the different ways of relating to realities and fictions, of believing in fictions and the realities they simulate, with more or less distance and detachment, are very closely linked to the different possible positions in social space and, consequently, bound up with the systems of dispositions (*habitus*) characteristic of the different classes and class fractions. Taste classifies, and it classifies the classifier. Social subjects, classified by their classifications, distinguish themselves by the distinctions they make, between the beautiful and the ugly, the distinguished and the vulgar, in which their position in the objective classifications is expressed or betrayed.[60]

Bourdieu's prose—complex, erudite, short on concrete examples, and here translated from the original French—is not always graceful or easy to follow, but when he wants to, he can sum himself up in a sentence as terse and thought-provoking as a Confucian epigram. *Taste classifies, and it classifies the classifier.* Bourdieu expands the tidy dictionary definition of taste as "aesthetic discernment in art or literature or conduct,"[61] by examining how readily taste is appropriated into the individual struggle for influence and power (in short, into the struggle for "distinction" within one's field), and the ways in which taste defines and reinforces differences (or "distinctions") in social class:

Nothing more clearly affirms one's "class," nothing more infallibly classifies, than tastes in music... For a bourgeois world which conceives its relation to the populace in terms of the relationship of the soul to the body, "insensitivity to music" doubtless represents a particularly unavowable form of materialist coarseness... Music represents the most radical and most absolute form of the negation of the world, and especially the social world, which the bourgeois ethos tends to demand of all forms of art.[62]

Bourdieu describes a "bourgeois world" of music in which European art music, or classical music, is the sole unquestionably "legitimate" form. Although other musics are admitted a certain "middle-brow" quality or "popular" appeal, they will never attain full "legitimate" status. On the other hand, jazz, along with cinema and the works of certain songwriters, is an art which "the most self-assured aesthetes can combine with the most legitimate of the arts that are still in the process of legitimation."[63] In other words, some people with "legitimate" tastes will accept jazz as a "high-brow" art form, on a par with classical music, although some of them only do so in order to deliberately distinguish themselves from prevailing opinions—in other words, to achieve distinction among their peers.

This positioning of jazz agrees with the dynamics we can observe in the jazz field of 1959. An overriding question was, is jazz as *good* as classical music? The esteemed Duke Ellington had already described jazz as "America's classical music," but as a black American himself, Ellington was not a member of the classical hegemony, and certainly not one of the gatekeepers who decided admittance to its exclusive circles. But an ongoing discourse, implicit in the discussions of Third Stream music such as the above comments by Schuller and Russell, outlined exactly the tensions between exclusion and legitimation that Bourdieu referred to in his references to jazz.

Taste, then, is one of the battery of assets, potent and valuable within the field of cultural production, that Bourdieu refers to as *cultural capital*.

CAPITAL

Within the arts, cultural capital can be defined as what one *knows* about one's chosen field: the knowledge of the genre's history, the background that enables one to interpret the codes implicit in a work, and perhaps most importantly, the command of the language used by members of the field. The possession of cultural capital is vital to the acquisition of *symbolic capital*, which "refers to degree of accumulated prestige, celebrity, consecration or honour and is founded on a dialectic of knowledge... and recognition."[64]

Only in certain circumstances can symbolic and cultural capital be converted into economic capital. In general, in other words, you can't make any money from them. Instead, a major item of trade among social groups is, in Randal Johnson's words:

> symbolic power based on diverse forms of capital which are not reducible to economic capital. Academic capital, for example, derives from formal education and can be measured by degrees or diplomas held. Linguistic capital concerns an agent's linguistic competence measured in relation to a specific linguistic market where often unrecognized power relations are at stake.

Two forms of capital are particularly important in the field of cultural production. *Symbolic capital* refers to degree of accumulated prestige, celebrity, consecration or honour and is founded on a dialectic of knowledge and recognition. *Cultural capital* concerns forms of cultural knowledge, competences or dispositions. Bourdieu defines cultural capital as a form of knowledge, an internalized code or a cognitive acquisition which equips the social agent with empathy towards, appreciation for or competence in deciphering cultural relations and cultural artifacts. He suggests that "a work of art has meaning and interest only for someone who possesses the cultural competence, that is, the code, into which it is encoded."[65] The possession of this code, or cultural capital, is accumulated through a long process of acquisition or inculcation which includes the pedagogical action of the family or group members (family education), educated members of the social formation (diffuse education) and social institutions (institutionalized education).

Possession of economic capital does not *necessarily* imply possession of cultural or symbolic capital, and vice versa. Bourdieu, in fact, analyzes the field of cultural production as an "economic world reversed" based on a "winner loses" logic, since economic success (in literary terms, for example, writing a best seller) may well signal a barrier to specific consecration and symbolic power.[66]

However, within a cultural field there can be many different kinds of relationships between cultural capital and economic capital.

FIELD

Many of the forces that came to bear around the Five Spot in November 1959 can be identified in Bourdieu's essay, "Field of Power, Literary Field and Habitus."[67] Here Bourdieu identifies, among other things, the "entirely recent historical inventions" of the writer and the artist as dependent on the constitution of an artistic "field." [68]

> What do I mean by "field"? As I use the term, a field is a separate social universe having its own laws of functioning independent of those of politics and the economy… The literary field (one may also speak of the artistic field, the philosophical field, etc.) is an independent social universe with its own laws of functioning, its specific relations of force, its dominants and its dominated, and so forth… [Within the field] there accumulates a particular form of capital and… relations of force of a particular type are exerted.[69]

Each artistic field is an "independent universe" whose members, even though they clash and compete for dominance, define themselves (and may even depend for their livelihoods) on the amount of cultural capital they possess, and are defined by other members according to the amount of symbolic capital (tangible, though not monetary, evidence of cultural capital—awards, publications, reviews, etc.) they have accumulated.

BOURDIEU'S THREE ARTISTIC POSITIONS

All members of an artistic field possess cultural capital to some degree, but no one's amount is exactly equal. All are struggling to gain more capital, or at least to maintain what they have, and the terrain is competitive, even combative. The battle for cultural capital is a battle for power—a battle for dominant positions within the field.

It is also a battle for survival. The more one is able to convert one's cultural capital to symbolic capital, the greater are one's chances of eventually extracting, or at least generating, economic capital from one's artistic enterprises. The music's most enthusiastic listeners, if not themselves musicians, write reviews, produce concerts, and start record companies. If they do not always make money from these enterprises, at least they gain symbolic capital, and as their personal capital accumulates, they gain the power to imbue others with symbolic capital. A sufficiently large accumulation of symbolic capital occasionally elicits a breakthrough in economic capital—for musicians, club gigs, concerts, record contracts and (in more recent years) arts grants, or awards that include cash prizes. For critics, paid reviewing work, a book contract that offers an advance, perhaps workshops or teaching engagements. For promoters and producers, the occasional concert or record that makes a clear profit. For any member of the field, an academic degree carries a certain amount of symbolic capital, that will vary in worth according to a host of different factors.

However, many members of an artistic field subsidize their participation with work in other fields. This enables them to maintain the integrity of the "economic field reversed," in which financial gain is downgraded, despised, repudiated and on rare occasions, even refused when offered (when a member's financial gain might compromise his or her position within the field). *Position* is essential. In fact, position is everything. In *The Field of Cultural Production,* Bourdieu points out that an artistic field is "a field of positions and a field of position-takings."[70] There are three major positions available to the artist:

1) Social art. "The partisans of social art... demand that literature fulfill a social or political function."

2) Bourgeois art. "The partisans of 'bourgeois art'... are closely and directly tied to the dominant class by their lifestyle and their system of values, and they receive, in addition to significant material benefits... all the symbols of bourgeois honour..."[71]

3) Art for art's sake. "Thus the defenders of art for art's sake occupy a central but structurally ambiguous position in the field which... compels them to think of themselves, on the aesthetic as well as the political level, in opposition to the 'bourgeois artists'... and in opposition to the 'social artists'... As a result, the members of this group are led to form contradictory images of the groups they oppose as well as of themselves... they can simultaneously or successively identify with a glorified working class or with a new aristocracy of the spirit."[72]

His remarks on the role of the avant garde depict the history of a given field as:

The struggle between the established figures and the young challengers... The agents engaged in the struggle are both contemporaries—precisely by virtue of the struggle which synchronizes them—and separated by time and in respect of time... The emergence of a group capable of "making an epoch" by imposing a new, advanced position is accompanied by a displacement of the structure of temporally hierarchized positions opposed within a given field; each of them moves a step down the temporal hierarchy which is at the same time a social hierarchy; the avant garde is separated by a generation from the consecrated avant garde which is itself separated by another generation from the avant garde that was already consecrated when it made its own entry into the field. Each author, school or work which "makes its mark" displaces the whole series of earlier authors, schools or works.[73]

A key word in this passage is *consecrated*. "Consecration" is the process by which an artist who newly arrives from outside of the field, or who is already allotted a low position in its hierarchy, achieves substantial status within it. It is a process whereby the value of one's symbolic capital is inarguably confirmed. In the arts, Bourdieu recognizes a range of "consecrating agents," from "academies, museums, learned societies and the educational system" to "literary circles, critical circles, salons, and small groups surrounding a famous author or associating with a publisher, a review or a literary or artistic magazine."[74]

Such "relations of force" were very much at work in the reception of the Ornette Coleman Quartet's music in the jazz "field" of 1959. Coleman's music, and the heat of the controversy around it, generated a wealth of accounts—reviews, interviews, anecdotes and historical analyses—of this time and place. Because of this, the forces that Bourdieu depicts as working implicitly within and around artistic fields—often at a salon's corner tables, within an art gallery's mailing list, or behind the closed doors of a record company or book publisher—can be seen clearly at work. The agents of these forces work to further the music's consecration, or to resist it; they allocate or deny symbolic capital; they angle, elbow or dicker to elevate their own artistic position within the jazz hierarchy.

SIX

The Culture of the Jazz Club

In their roles as meeting places, the cafés, nightclubs and bars of Greenwich Village had spawned a unique local culture, a regionally distinct urban intellectual field, by bringing together artists and artistic mediators (gallery owners, editors, scholars, critics) from different disciplines. Within this culture the famous mingled with the infamous and the unfamous, the celebrity with the fan, the rich with the poor, the hip with the square. This culture also served as an important meeting place for black people and whites.

Robert K. McMichael offers an interesting perspective on the dynamics of the presentation of jazz, usually played by black musicians, in these venues:

> The fact that whites owned the majority of jazz clubs is significant, and often mitigated or limited the extent to which musicians could practise their craft freely. However, it is worth considering the very existence of an improvisatory African-American art form in a white-owned commercial space something of a radical (or at least postmodern) configuration, at least insofar as the tension between capitalist market forces and racially integrated but African-American improvisatory and antiphonal practices often dramatically interrupts dominant racist social codes.[75]

McMichael also quotes from Charles Mingus' autobiography *Beneath the Underdog,* and identifies a club Mingus calls "The Fast Buck" as the Five Spot circa 1959:

> The club is definitely the place this season for society and college girls from New York and out-of-town who want to have a fling at life via the bandstand or the single male customers who press around the bar and it's nothing wild to walk in on a crowded night and find Mingus at a table with half a dozen girls huddled around him or sitting on his knees or him perching on theirs... These days

Charles feels wholly free and not only as good as any white people but better than most and he's found a musical home, a place to play for people who really seem to want to hear.[76]

McMichael concludes that "the musicians as well as the audience were conscious of and interested in the cultivation of an integrationist subculture."[77]

The jazz club of 1959, then, was a place where racial tensions between black and white were ignored, sublimated, or enacted in more subtle forms (as exemplified by Mingus' adoring coterie of white women, the jazz club milieu enabled whites to pay homage to black artists, to enact a liberating, if temporary, reversal of the roles allocated to them in American society). This could be said to be true of the jazz field as a whole: it had an independent identity as a field in itself, but it also provided numerous intersections where the (predominantly white) members of different fields—poetry, *belles lettres,* painting, classical music—could congregate and in doing so, publicly display their liberal humanism in regard to black American culture. From its opening until well into the 1960s, the Five Spot Café was one of the busier of these intersections.

Its importance as an arena of interactions, in which participants gained different degrees of cachet by displaying their participation in the jazz field, can be especially understood through the presence of Norman Mailer (1923–) and James Baldwin (1924–1988). Both were young writers who had made names for themselves through fiction as well as essays and criticism. They were also both native New Yorkers, although as Baldwin pointed out, "I am a black boy from the Harlem streets, and Norman is a middle-class Jew."[78] Their attendance at the Five Spot gave them a place in the jazz field, but they were prominent members of another artistic field, the New York literary field.[79]

NORMAN MAILER

Although Norman Mailer was already making his influence felt in literary books and journals, he also made his opinions known within the jazz field—an artistic field in which, although he neither played, presented or wrote about jazz, he nevertheless felt a personal stake. For example, Buell Neidlinger, Cecil Taylor's bassist at the Five Spot, claims that a Taylor residency there was curtailed by influential members of the jazz community because of Mailer's loud championing of Taylor's music over that of Thelonious Monk, who was playing at a rival club.[80] Even if Mailer was not a jazz stakeholder professionally, he spent enough time in jazz clubs that eventually even the Five Spot became an active part of his writing career. Mailer's *Esquire* coverage of the 1960 Democratic National Convention came about through a chance meeting with *Esquire* editor Clay Felker in the Five Spot on a busy spring night (in fact, the dates indicate it was probably during a Coleman engagement) when Joe Termini seated Felker at Mailer's table.[81]

If there was a "voice of the times" in the bustling New York City intellectual community at the end of the 1950s, it was Norman Mailer. In print and in live discourse, he was loud, arresting, controversial and occasionally brilliant. His influence was pervasive, and it is possible that examples of his writing can give us clues to the context in which critics (by and large white critics, except for Baraka) received Ornette Coleman's debut.

Mailer's writing had established him as a kind of link between the ecstatic, anti-establishment literature of the Beats, such as Jack Kerouac and Allen Ginsberg, and the equally passionate, but more precise liberalism of writers like Baldwin and Gore Vidal. In the month that Coleman opened at the Five Spot, Mailer's "The Mind of an Outlaw" appeared in *Esquire*—an essay that characterized modern writers (especially Mailer himself) as anti-establishment outsiders.

Even more significant was "The White Negro," an excerpt from Mailer's new book *Advertisements for Myself* that had appeared in the magazine he edited, *Dissent,* earlier in the year.[82] Passages from "The White Negro" display a view of jazz—and a view of venues such as the Five Spot—that to an extent pervaded the era's intellectual life:

> But the presence of Hip as a working philosophy in the sub-worlds
> of American life is probably due to jazz, and its knifelike entrance
> into culture, its subtle but so penetrating influence on an avant-

garde generation... In such places as Greenwich Village, a *ménage-à-trois* was completed—the bohemian and the juvenile delinquent came face-to-face with the Negro, and the hipster was a fact in American life...

For jazz is orgasm, it is the music of orgasm, good orgasm and bad, and so it spoke across a nation, it had the communication of art even where it was watered, perverted, corrupted, and almost killed, it spoke in no matter what laundered popular way of instantaneous existential states to which some whites could respond, it was indeed a communication by art because it said, "I feel this, and now you do too."[83]

Mailer's point of view was unapologetically essentialist: at the same time that he paid homage to alleged African-American spontaneity, sexuality, and primitivism, he was interested in these forces primarily as muses for his own "avant-garde generation" of white artists. Although one might excuse the "White Negro" perspective as a white intellectual's sincere attempt to embrace (his own concept of) black culture on the same terms that he embraced his own, it is worth questioning the extent to which it encourages a misinterpretation and even a total misreading of black music. As Ingrid Monson writes,

To the extent that well-meaning white Americans have confused the most "transgressive" aspects of African-American culture with its true character, they fall into the trap of viewing blackness as absence. Whether conceived as an absence of morality or of bourgeois pretensions, this view of blackness, paradoxically, buys into the historical legacy of primitivism and its concomitant exoticism of the "Other."[84]

Monson traces the myth of black "hipness" through the writing of Mezz Mezzrow—a white clarinetist in New Orleans and early swing styles who claimed a heartfelt identification with black culture—and through the emergence of bebop. In every case, she finds that intellectual curiosity, the systematic exploration of new ideas and the cultivation of discipline among black jazz musicians is misinterpreted by white enthusiasts:

> Different observers, it seems, chose to emphasize different aspects of bebop according to their investment in particular images and associations of blackness and music. In their recollections, the principal musical participants stress the intellectuality, artistry, and social consciousness of the musical movement. [Bebop drummer] Kenny Clarke recalls: "It was the most intelligent phase of our music... There was a message in our music. Whatever you go into, go into it *intelligently*. As simple as that." By contrast, Mailer saw in the hip African-American the true existentialist/hedonist who counteracted death by taking an "uncharted journey into the rebellious imperatives of the self," with particular attention to the pleasures of the body.[85]

Given the high profile of Mailer's writing at the time—certainly other journalists, including jazz journalists, would have been aware of it—it seems possible that in his romanticized discourse, Mailer was voicing expectations that certain white listeners were bringing to black music. These expectations were that jazz would offer more than just passing enjoyment; in fact, that it had the potential to be even more profound an art form than classical music. Certainly, any serious jazz lover would agree, but these particular listeners also cultivated the perspective that, both in the primacy it gave to improvisation and in the "hipness" of its origins in African-American culture, jazz was virtually an embodiment of elemental forces. Within this perspective, jazz mystically entwined and merged sexual desire, the urge to individual freedom and dignity, and the creative impulse itself into a single, and singular, musical voice.[86]

These expectations were rarely expressed when jazz music was defined by its actual practitioners. As Monson writes of her interviews with African-American jazz musicians, "I found that most emphasized discipline and responsibility as the keys to performing at a level that meets the jazz community's standards of spontaneity and soulfulness."[87]

It is nevertheless useful to keep these quotes from "The White Negro" in mind when trying to grasp the expectations of critics as they approached the music of Ornette Coleman. Doing so helps to illuminate, among other things, the clash of agendas between what musicians saw as important, and what was valued by jazz critics and influential jazz listeners of the time—and to understand the passions that flared when these expectations were projected onto this new music.

JAMES BALDWIN

Despite his pride in his African-American heritage and culture, beginning in his teens the writer James Baldwin found himself drawn from uptown Harlem to lower Manhattan's Greenwich Village. He did so following a line of thought which although too infrequent to be called a movement, Jon Panish has called "a pattern for alienated or disaffected African-Americans to follow, part of which included, at least, contact with the Village's more enlightened Euro American bohemians."[88]

Although Panish dates the beginning of this particular link between Harlem and the Village to the 1920s, he writes that "the pattern was firmly established by the late 1940s and early 1950s," less by writers than by jazz musicians, notably the iconic bebop alto saxophonist Charlie Parker.

As with other black artists in predominantly white village society, Baldwin found that, although his race in itself gave him a status that was perhaps special rather than equal, he was at least encouraged in his literary interests.[89] His background gave him a unique perspective on the dynamics of a Lower Manhattan meeting place catering to a mostly white clientele, such as the Five Spot, in his comparison of Harlem ("uptown") and Lower Manhattan ("downtown") night life. If the black club is a happier place, Baldwin says, it is not because black Americans are a "happy" people, but because:

> No one gives a damn, and this allows everyone to be himself—at the club. No one gives a damn because they know exactly how rough it is out there, when the club gates close. And while they are dancing and listening to the music and drinking and joking and

laughing, with all their finery on, and looking so bold and free, they know who enters, who leaves, and on what errands: they are aware of the terrible and unreachable forces which yet rule their lives.

Well, the Negro is not happy in his place, and white people aren't happy in their place, either—two very intimately related facts—but the unhappiness of white people seems never to rattle and resound more fiercely than in their pleasure mills. The world that mainly frequents white nightclubs seems afflicted with a strange uncertainty as to whether or not they are really having fun—they keep peeping at each other in order to find out. One's aware, in an eerie way, that there are barriers which must not be crossed, and that by these invisible barriers everyone is mesmerized. But it is quite impossible to discover where, in action, these barriers are to be found; nothing matches the abandon of those struggling to be free of invisible chains, who wish, at the same time, to remain socially safe. And nothing matches the joylessness, either... White people are isolated from each other in their nightclubs as they are all over America, in their daily lives. The nightclub being no place to establish a human relationship, they walk out as untouched as they were when they walked in. It is this cumulative and grinding inability to reach out to others which makes nightclub life, downtown, so grim.[90]

On occasion Baldwin's writing, like Mailer's, had paid tribute to the power of African-American music and to the transcendent message of jazz, yet it conveyed an insider's view, shorn of Mailer's essentialism and certainly of any notion of "hipness." As a gay man and as a black man, Baldwin was compelled to step carefully, testing his welcome, into the Lower Manhattan venues where Mailer made his presence known so noisily. Eventually, each made his own place in his own way within those circles. Simply as a black man, Baldwin's relationship to the music and to the milieu of the Lower Manhattan jazz scene was very different from Mailer's. For example, both men became well-acquainted with Miles Davis, but where Mailer's relationship with the trumpeter was tense and competitive, Baldwin and Davis formed a warm, lifelong friendship.

THE JAZZ CLUB AND ITS AUDIENCE

In 1959 it was common for a group's club engagement to last for at least two weeks and sometimes more. Each week's performances generally lasted from Tuesday to Sunday with a matinee added on Saturday afternoon, and as Coleman did at the Five Spot, the musicians played from 9:00 p.m. until 3:00 a.m. each night. It is easy to understand Coleman's complaint at the time, that the strain of this schedule interfered with the creativity that was his ostensible appeal.[91]

However, until his new fame brought him to the Monterey Festival and New York's Town Hall in 1959, Coleman had only played in clubs and, in his early Texas days, in dance halls. As he developed his own style, his music became increasingly out of sync with the spirit of these venues:

> Drummer Mel Lewis, who gigged in and around Los Angeles in the mid-1950s, recalls an engagement with Bill Holman, who was an early supporter of Coleman's music: "We were working over at the Jazz Cellar on La Palmas, and one night Ornette Coleman came and sat in with us. You never saw a club empty out so fast. The woman who ran the club told us that if we let him sit in again, we were fired. The very next night, who comes in but John Lewis and Gunther Schuller. They want to hear Ornette with the band. Well, we let him sit in again, and the club emptied out again. This time she fires us."[92]

Paul Bley also describes how the Hillcrest's predominantly black, working-class audience reacted when Coleman and Don Cherry first performed with his band:

> Several things happened almost at once. The audience en masse got up, leaving their drinks on the table and on the bar, and headed for the door. The club literally emptied as soon as the band began playing.
>
> For the duration of that gig, if you were driving down Washington Boulevard past the Hillcrest Club you could always tell

if the band was on the bandstand or not. If the street was full of the audience holding drinks in front of the club, the band was playing. If the audience was in the club, it was intermission. [93]

Bley's quartet with Dave Pike had built a good relationship with the club owner and with a large audience of regulars. Obviously the new configuration with Coleman and Cherry was no longer fulfilling the same function.[94] Although still based in steady jazz time, the music's angular melodies and dissonant voicings, the bittersweet, vocalized exchanges of the two horns, and the unpredictable twists and turns of the group's improvisations were a world apart from the more conventional aural background the group had supplied as a piano/vibraphone quartet.

At the Five Spot in the new bohemia of the East Village, one might expect that the audience reaction would be more urbane, more informed, and more tolerant—indeed, encouraging—of new developments. Indeed, to some extent because of the musical controversy he had generated in the media, every night that Coleman's quartet played at the Five Spot became a kind of spectacle, drawing an audience quite different from the audience at the Hillcrest the previous year. The character of Coleman's audience at the Five Spot was so distinctive, and its expectations so different from that of the usual jazz audience, that in the pages of the British journal *New Statesman,* Eric Hobsbawm raised serious questions about Coleman and his listeners. While recognizing that Coleman was "a deeply impressive artist," he asked:

But who has recognized him? The public at the Five Spot is overwhelmingly young, white, and intellectual or bohemian. Here are the jazz fans (white or coloured) with the "Draft Stevenson" buttons, lost over their $1.50 beer. If Coleman were to blow in Small's Paradise in Harlem, it would clear the place in five minutes. Musicians such as he are, it seems, as cut off from the common listeners among their people as Webern is from the public at the Filey Butlin's. They depend on those who are themselves alienated, the internal emigrants of America.[95]

Hobsbawm's plaint acknowledges a change that had already taken place in the jazz field: although most of the music's creators were black Americans, it was no longer especially a music played for black American audiences (although the extent to which it ever had been is a weighty subject in itself). Especially as Hobsbawm was a visitor from another country where jazz audiences had always been predominantly white, it is interesting to speculate as to why he would place such importance on the audience demographic. Perhaps as a visitor he saw jazz less as a subset of a larger field of "American music," and more as a subset of the field of "African-American culture."

Hobsbawm clearly is referring to the audience as much more than passive consumers who empower the music with their paid attendance. They define the music itself and imbue it with cultural value. In effect, they become a constituency whose very presence is a demonstration of support; to take the analogy a step further, a constituency who have agreed to let the musicians to represent them. Towards this relationship, Hobsbawm's doubts are about *authenticity;* about the extent to which the Coleman quartet actually represented their audience, and vice versa.

Hobsbawm, despite his misgivings, came out on the side of Coleman's music. Overall he found it shocking, even unpleasant, but irresistible. He admitted that "the unforgettable thing... is the passion with which he blows. I have heard nothing like it in modern jazz since Parker."[96]

Regardless of who actually came to the Five Spot, Coleman drew so well that the two-week engagement stretched to ten weeks, lasting until the end of January 1960. Two months later, on April 5, the quartet (with Edward Blackwell replacing Higgins on drums) returned for another engagement, this time staying for four months.

CONTEMPORARY ACCOUNTS OF THE FIVE SPOT'S JAZZ "FIELD"

A Saroyan bar-and-grill at the sound end of Cooper Square... the Five Spot is long and narrow, with a bar, sheltered by a fringed canopy, running down most of one wall; three gold-coloured macelike objects suspended from a maroon ceiling; and the rest of the wall space spattered with posters and programs of various sorts.

— Whitney Balliett, 1959[97]

A plain Third Avenue bar, at the foot of Cooper Square, that took on jazz in the mid-fifties simply by adding a piano and a small bandstand. It was small and unpretentious and you could see and hear from anywhere in the room. As a result, it was intricately awash with music and reaction, reaction and music.

— Balliett, 1963[98]

Perhaps we can better understand the impact of Coleman's debut if we look more closely at the Five Spot itself. There is a wealth of documentation from the time and place, but little of it is as concise as Balliett's descriptions above.

By the late 1950s, the image of the bereted bohemian or "beatnik" was seen again and again on record and magazine covers, on television and in Hollywood films. A popular trope, this image pervades the work of journalists who felt the Five Spot was best described via its audience:

The Five Spot, one of New York's more *outré* jazz clubs, usually attracts a fairly wild-looking crowd of jazz aficionados. College girls in shorts rub shoulders with long-haired painters in mottled dungarees. Village girls in leotards, men in sweaters and leather jackets—their eyes shaded by dark glasses—sailors, cadets, and the Madison Avenue cool crowd, have all made the Five Spot their own. It is home for both the "beatnik" and the serious jazz student.[99]

It was common enough in the era's journalism to treat the mixed cast of Village bohemia as a novelty. However, in doing so Robert Kotlowitz of *Harper's* managed to make some serious points. Certainly in terms of Bourdieu's "three artistic positions," it is interesting to read Robert Kotlowitz's description of the audience that filled the Five Spot for Thelonious Monk's extended residency in 1961:

What Monk's audience thinks of him depends on which audience is being talked about. There are three.

One is in attendance because it has gathered that it is the hip thing to do... Jazz offers swollen legends of narcotics, of drink, race guilt, and violence, bearing a strangely attractive aura of sadness and pain. For the "hippies," it means an evening's brush with emotional anarchy for the price of a beer.

A second audience comes because it has heard that Monk is a character... For this audience, he is a spectacle; it is sheerest coincidence that a little music is thrown in.

The third audience, young, ardent, and often bearded without being beat, will come to a nightclub for a Monk performance, but it won't drink very much. It is loyal, intense, and responsive to the music, which is what it comes to hear.[100]

The writer clearly observes and defines the three artistic positions that Bourdieu was to define two decades later. The first audience is attracted to the music as *social art*. They are less interested in aesthetic experience than in social significance, and want no more than a detached, even voyeuristic exposure to the music's "swollen legends of narcotics, of drink, race guilt, and violence." The second audience comes searching for *bourgeois art*, for entertainment: to see Monk dance, wear funny hats and otherwise be a "spectacle." The writer most clearly approves of the third audience: "loyal, intense, and responsive," this audience concentrates on the music itself, regarding it as *art for art's sake*.

Having played with Coleman in Los Angeles, Paul Bley was an enthusiastic listener at the Five Spot and, as a veteran performer himself, a connoisseur of bandstand politics. In his own way, he describes Coleman's debut clearly in terms of artistic position. In the custom of the day, Coleman's quartet alternated sets with a group called the Jazztet, a "sextet that sounds like a big band," according to their publicity.[101] The group was led by trumpeter Art Farmer and tenor saxophonist Benny Golson, with trombonist Curtis Fuller, pianist McCoy Tyner, Addison Farmer on bass and Dave Bailey on drums.[102] This is how Bley describes the pairing of the Jazztet's music with Coleman's:

The week before Ornette came [the Jazztet] sounded like a very modern, Horace Silver-type arranged band: beautiful aesthetics, with all the rough points ironed out, slick, smooth. Ornette played one set and turned them into Guy Lombardo.[103]

Again we have a description of the displacement of artistic position within the field: a group that was, if not avant-garde, certainly "modern," lost stature upon Coleman's entry into the jazz field. In Bley's description, Coleman's music stripped the Jazztet of the potential to be regarded as "art for art's sake," and relegated them to the status of bourgeois art.

SEVEN

The Musicians and the Critics

In order to accept the concept of cultural capital and symbolic capital, it is fair to ask how this capital becomes imbued with value. Although one's impulse might be to denote all value within a work of art as the product of the artist alone, Bourdieu attributes the creation of artistic value to all members of an artistic field.

As an example from the jazz field, we could take Miles Davis playing his composition *Kind of Blue*. The *sound* that came from Davis' trumpet is completely his creation as composer, interpreter and improviser. However, Davis' intentions and opinions as to how much that sound should be valued as *art* are only a small part of the eventual consensus as to the value of that sound—a consensus arrived at by the efforts of many. Value is added by the presenter who deems that sound worth presenting in a club or concert hall, and by the producer who believes that a recording of that sound can be promoted and sold as a work of art. Value is added by the audience who pays to hear that sound; whether they applaud each solo, or wait silently until the end of each tune, or talk while the music is playing, they have all invested in the belief that they gain something from association with that sound. Value is added by the scholar who can place that sound in the context of the jazz trumpeters who came before and after Davis. Value is added by any listener who acknowledges the worth of the recording of *Kind of Blue* by buying it. Whether they play it only to themselves, play it for friends, or buy it and never play it at all, in every case, it is their choice, their decision that has imbued that sound with value as a work of art.

Bourdieu attributes to the critic a major role in the creation of value:

> The production of discourse (critical, historical, etc.) about the work of art is one of the conditions of production of the work. Every critical affirmation contains, on the one hand, a recognition of the value of the work which occasions it, which is thus desig-

nated as a worthy object of legitimate discourse... and on the other hand an affirmation of its own legitimacy. All critics declare not only their judgement of the work but also their claim to the right to talk about it and judge it. In short, they take part in a struggle for the monopoly of legitimate discourse about the work of art, and consequently in the production of the value of the work of art.[104]

THE OLD VERSUS THE NEW

Bernard Gendron identifies jazz criticism as an ongoing conflict between two opposing sets of values—two sets of antagonists who were originally identified and labeled as such during "the first jazz war" fought between New Orleans revivalists (known to their detractors as "moldy figs") and modernists (advocates of the new "swing" styles) in the 1940s.[105] Their heated debates introduced to jazz the type of aesthetic discourse within which the Coleman controversy was conducted. As Gendron writes:

The unity of this new aesthetic discourse was a "unity in dispersion," to use Foucault's phrase—that is, a unity that propagated discursive opposition, that created points of discursive repulsion. As such, it was organized primarily around a group of interconnected binary oppositions: *art–commerce, authenticity–artificiality, swing–jazz, European–native, folk culture–refined culture, technique–affect, modern–traditional, black–white, fascism–communism,* and *right wing–left wing.*[106]

Bearing in mind the controversy around Coleman and the emerging "free jazz" style, one might also add to these binaries *improvised–composed* and *freedom–oppression.*

Gendron describes how these discursive practices became entrenched during the first "jazz war" between revivalists and swing modernists, and were carried over intact into the second "jazz war," where swing now represented stodgy tradition, and bebop the new, threatening avant garde. Gendron points out that:

The revivalists were as much "modernists" as were their swing adversaries. They simply accentuated certain tendencies of the "modernist" impulse at the expense of others. We need to remember, for example, that the concepts of the *folkloric* and the *primitive* were crucially involved in the "modernist" practices of Picasso, Bartók, Milhaud, and the Surrealists, while the notion of *reactionary* and art/commerce dichotomy entered crucially into the avant-garde terminologies of opprobrium.[107]

Largely because of the discursive language defined and deployed in the "jazz wars," by 1959 jazz criticism had evolved a set of expectations regarding the music, and a way of perceiving and discussing it, that was, in Gendron's words, "lifted out of the various European avant-garde and modernist discourses."[108]

It seems likely that such a *habitus,* certainly among New York jazz critics circa 1959, was also influenced by the era's literary writers. To start with, they shared a common geography in the neighbourhoods of the East and Greenwich Village, a sprawling intellectual milieu in which the memberships of the literary and jazz fields met and overlapped. Such a confluence, and influence, is certainly implied in first-hand accounts of the Five Spot audience of the time, where jazz critics such as Nat Hentoff and Martin Williams mingled with literary writers, including Mailer and Kerouac. If the fields themselves overlapped, it is not unreasonable to speculate that the agendas of the fields' members overlapped as well, and certainly that the discursive practices described by Gendron were very much at work.

Discussing critical reactions to Miles Davis' music in the 1950s, John Szwed writes, "Jazz critics were high modernists, looking for originality, influence, a certain toughness of self-expression in their heroes."[109] In writing about the same period—the declining years of bebop—Scott DeVeaux has identified the work of "a shifting (and often uneasy) coalition of musicians and critics" who campaigned to position jazz "on the far side of the 'Great Divide' separating art in the modernist mold from 'an increasingly consuming and engulfing mass culture.'"[110]

Of course individuality, tough and even idiosyncratic self-expression, and an identification with "art in the modernist mold," rather than with the products of mass culture, are precisely the positions that Norman Mailer attributed to the hipster in "The White Negro." Taken together, they can be summed up under a single label: *authenticity.*

Gendron identifies authenticity as an important part of the 1940s revivalist–swing debate, and in fact it also played a big part in early critical assessments of Coleman. Authenticity is, if anything, resolutely anti-commercial; as Bourdieu writes, "A heretical break with the prevailing artistic traditions proves its claim to authenticity by its disinterestedness."[111] A key word here is "prevailing"; a recidivist movement can be just as aggressive, just as heretical, just as disdainful of the status quo, as an avant-garde movement.

The "high modernist" search for authenticity can clearly be seen at work in jazz criticism at the time of Coleman's debut.

For example, during the first week of Coleman's Five Spot engagement, the *New York Times* critic John S. Wilson reviewed a Town Hall jazz concert that included sets by Chico Hamilton and Dave Brubeck—both respected artists who had experimented with classical forms (Hamilton's quintet, uniquely among jazz groups, even included a cellist). Both had achieved critical praise as well as popular success. In reviewing the evening's performances, however, Wilson found that "the only jazz of merit... came in two brief solos by Mr. Hamilton's versatile reedman, Eric Dolphy, one on alto saxophone and the other a remarkably virtuosic and swinging spree on bass clarinet."[112]

At the time Dolphy (1928–1964) was still based in Los Angeles, where he had been acquainted with Coleman (and evidently joined the jazz majority in dismissing him) during the 1950s.[113] Dolphy, however, did not share Coleman's problems of acceptance with other musicians, because of his thorough conventional training, his excellent sight-reading, and his willingness and ability to improvise within song forms.[114] Nevertheless, toward the end of the decade Dolphy's techniques on saxophone, bass clarinet and flute were becoming increasingly vocalized, full of unexpected manipulations of pitch and timbre and a freeness of phrasing. In the next few years, he collaborated with Coleman as well as such innovators as Charles Mingus and John Coltrane.

It is noteworthy that in a concert featuring some of the era's most successful and acclaimed jazz artists, a critic for a major newspaper would credit a player as challenging as Dolphy with providing "the only jazz of merit." Perhaps this confirms Szwed's description of the critical search for "heroes" rather than entertainers, as well as an example of what DeVeaux terms the positioning of jazz as "art in the modernist mold" rather than as a part of "mass culture."

This agenda can be seen again in the December 1959 *Down Beat*, an issue of the magazine that would have been on the newsstands at the time of Coleman's Five Spot debut. Among the record reviews, respected jazz musicians get short shrift from a range of well-known jazz critics. Jimmy Cleveland's all-star sextet, claims critic Don DeMicheal, "rarely gets off the ground." Buddy Collette's four-flute record is "all but a waste of time," writes Ralph Gleason (later a co-founder of *Rolling Stone* magazine).[115]

At first, DeMicheal seems prepared to dismiss Ornette Coleman's second Contemporary record, "Tomorrow is the Question." The reviewer takes note of the music's "wild, incoherent solos... marked by extremely bad intonation and sloppy execution." However, rather than dismissing the record for its wildness and incoherence, DeMicheal rates the record as "astonishing"—a record that "must be listened to many times... Coleman may be the next great influence." In contrast to the responses to Cleveland and Collette, DeMicheal seems to be saying that Coleman may not be competent—but at least he is original, at least he is *authentic.* The same devaluation of what one might call "professionalism" can also be read into Paul Bley's estimation of how the Farmer–Golson Jazztet fared in the new context implied by Coleman's music.

This modernist need for the transgressive, the authentic, even the primitive, pervades a subsequent *Down Beat* account of the press preview that the Termini brothers held at the Five Spot on the evening of Coleman's opening night. The need is so implicit that the writer, George

Hoefer, does not even find it necessary to discuss or describe the music itself. His perspective on the audience is quite different than that of Hobsbawm, or Kotlowitz, and he refers to the music only in terms of the extent to which it fulfills the modernist agenda: "Jazz can well use a new thrill, idea, or sound, something similar to what happened when a jaded swing era spawned Charlie Parker, Thelonious Monk and Dizzy Gillespie in the early 1940s."[116]

This agenda pervades the work of all four of these critics. "Ah conformity!" DeMicheal writes despairingly in his Jimmy Cleveland review. Coleman's record, on the other hand, "must be listened to many times." Part of the "high modernist" agenda was an aversion to "conformity," which Eric Lott has identified as part of "an American tradition of racial abdication."[117] On the other hand, because it was also accepted as a symptom of creative genius, "nonconformity" could be used to excuse a wide range of idiosyncratic, even aberrant behaviour. As Ingrid Monson writes, "To the extent that the romantic conception of the artist linked the notion of genius with madness and pathology, and entitled the artist to behave in an unorthodox manner as well, it opened an interpretive space in which supposedly negative social behaviours could be transformed into positive markers of artistic genius."[118]

It is revealing that Hoefer's review offers virtually no comment on how the music *sounded* to him as a listener. Instead, he follows his writer's intuition that his readers can best assess the music's value by surveying the reactions of the other artistic mediators in the audience. Hoefer's few references to the quartet's actual music are vague and casual—but his description of the clientele is thoroughly engaged:

> Some walked in and out before they could finish a drink, some sat mesmerized by the sound, others talked constantly to their neighbors at the table or argued with drink in hand at the bar. It was, for all this, the largest collection of VIPs the jazz world has seen in many a year. A sampling included John Hammond, John Mehegan, Marshall Stearns, Jack Lewis, Burt Korall, Eric Vogel (American correspondent for Germany's *Jazz Podium* magazine), Hsio Wen

Shih, Gunther Schuller, Symphony Sid Torin, Pete Long, Bob Reisner, and the Ertegun brothers...

This special preview for the press brought forth mixed-up comments:

"He'll change the entire course of jazz." "He's a fake." "He's a genius." "I can't say; I'll have to hear him a lot more times." "He has no form." "He swings like HELL." "I'm going home and listen to my Benny Goodman trios and quartets." "He's out, real far out." "I like him, but I don't have any idea what he is doing."

Finally, one a&r[119] man made the simple statement "I've got a recording date" and left.[120]

It is worth noting that, in order to impress the reader, Hoefer chooses the names of producers, educators, critics and broadcasters. Only two of these "very important persons" from the jazz world might actually be described as jazz musicians (pianist/educator John Mehegan and the British alto saxophonist Pete Long).

The list of vocations confirms Bourdieu's depiction of a "field of cultural production" in which, although not all the field's members actually produce the art, each of their efforts must conjoin to validate, to literally *substantiate* the art, to agree for their own sakes that it is indeed art.

In Bourdieu's terms, Coleman could have asked no better ticket of admission to a jazz field consisting of "positions and a field of position-takings" (*Down Beat* was the leading US jazz magazine, and Hoefer had been a contributor for over twenty years) than this confirmation that his art's importance would ultimately be determined by the positions taken towards it by the field's members.[121] In order to describe and define the music, all Hoefer needs to do is (A) establish that other influential field members attended the event and then (B) log the positions, pro and con, of a cross-section of these attendees, diplomatically refraining from naming each speaker or indeed, committing himself to a position of his own.

No superlatives were needed for the music itself when superlatives could be applied so readily to the event's clientele.

THE REACTIONS OF JAZZ MUSICIANS

The response to Coleman's music from New York's jazz musicians seems to have been, at least at first, overwhelmingly negative. One of the era's most progressive and proactive critics, Nat Hentoff, recorded some of their responses:[122]

> Roy Eldridge: "I think he's jiving, baby. He's putting everybody on."
>
> Coleman Hawkins: "Now, you know that I never like to criticize anyone publicly. Just say I think he needs seasoning. A lot of seasoning."
>
> Red Garland: "Nothing's happening... Coleman is faking. He's being very unfair to the public."[123]

Miles Davis went to the Five Spot accompanied by his sextet's tenor saxophonist, John Coltrane. Coltrane was intrigued, later played with Coleman privately, and was soon to follow many of Coleman's leads in developing his own music. It was Davis, however, riding the crest of a wave of critically acclaimed and commercially successful LPs, whose comments were picked up by the press: "Hell, just listen to what he writes and how he plays it," he said of Coleman. "If you're talking psychologically, the man is all screwed up inside."[124]

In these comments we can read an enactment of what Bourdieu would identify as a struggle between artistic generations:

> The structure of the field of cultural production is based on two fundamental and quite different oppositions: first, the opposition between the sub-field of restricted production and the sub-field of large-scale production, i.e. between two economies, two time-scales, two audiences, which endlessly produces and reproduces the negative existence of the sub-field of restricted production and its basic opposition to the bourgeois economic order; and secondly,

the opposition, within the sub-field of restricted production, between the consecrated avant garde and the avant garde, the established figures and the newcomers, i.e. between *artistic generations*, often only a few years apart, between the "young" and the "old," the "neo" and the "paleo," the "new" and the "outmoded," etc.; in short, between cultural orthodoxy and heresy.[125]

Appearing suddenly in a prestigious venue for modern jazz, Coleman was just such a newcomer, an un-consecrated avant-garde figure. He became a clear target for the opposition that Bourdieu identifies, and the focus of the conflict "between artistic generations, often only a few years apart," that Bourdieu describes. Seen in this light, perhaps we can better understand the vehemence of so many of Coleman's detractors among jazz musicians. Miles Davis, for example, was the reigning jazz star of the time. One can read in his comments on Coleman a possible bitterness at being displaced—sent down the ranks, as it were—from his prevailing, pre-eminent position. To do such a thing, Coleman's shortcomings must be more than just musical shortcomings; the man must be "all screwed up inside."

Milt Jackson, vibraphonist in the popular and respected Modern Jazz Quartet (which ironically, he co-led with Coleman's advocate John Lewis), stated that the music was "nothing—there's no such thing as free form."[126] Drummer Max Roach, a bebop pioneer and a successful leader and innovator in his own right, objected to the music so strongly that one night he followed Coleman into the Five Spot kitchen between sets, punched him in the mouth, and later harangued him from the street outside his apartment.[127]

It is worth noting that despite their initial revulsion, many of these musicians made sincere efforts to come to terms with this new music. Within a few years of Coleman's Five Spot debut, many of those who had rejected Coleman, perhaps with some qualifications, now accepted him, though often with some reservations. It seems possible that professional jazz musicians' thorough grounding in conventional harmony and the chord changes of the song form did not equip them for hearing— much less playing—this new music, and they needed time to rethink

Coleman's approach in terms of their own. Admittedly, once musicians have been schooled and experienced in navigating the more rigid constraints of the song form, it is perhaps not completely fair to expect them to immediately absorb the style pioneered by Coleman, with its shifting tonality, free rhythms and restless, dancelike exchange of voices.

By the following summer, Roach's antagonism had eased enough for him to play with Coleman at the rival Newport festival that Roach and Charles Mingus had organized.[128] Both the drummer's and Mingus' subsequent recordings introduced "free" elements that had not been heard before in their music; the same is true for Miles Davis, and certainly for John Coltrane. By 1962, even Coleman Hawkins and Shelly Manne felt permitted—perhaps even obliged—to insert a freely improvised tenor saxophone–drums duet into an album of jazz standards.[129]

Among musicians newly exposed to Ornette Coleman, there was a pattern of resistance, then acceptance. The resistance stage can be easily understood in terms of the impact of an avant-garde newcomer on the jazz field. In a "self-contained universe," where the most valued currency is symbolic capital, the avant garde occupies a high position, possessing a uniquely precious capital that cannot be shared until it is more widely understood.

Milt Jackson, an active member of the bebop generation in the 1940s when they *were* the jazz avant garde, was still "modern," but was associated already with the Modern Jazz Quartet's "cool," sedate brand of modernism, successfully marketed to predominantly white bourgeois audiences in concerts and the pricier nightclubs. It seems feasible to surmise that Jackson would not disdain or resist his relegation to the jazz field's "old guard." Such positioning would present no professional disadvantage, and would classify him along with artists he considered to be more rightfully his peers. Jackson's career was built primarily on his reputation as the finest vibraphonist in jazz, and Coleman's music was making no claims on that particular territory. With these factors taken together, it was just as easy for Jackson, having made his statements on Coleman's music, to withdraw, claiming no further investment in the controversy.

Davis, however, was the leading figure in what Bourdieu would term the consecrated avant garde. He had followed the protocols of apprenticeship, establishing his musical credentials working with such artists as Coleman Hawkins and Charlie Parker, who had long since been accepted into the canon of the jazz tradition. He had just recorded his ground-breaking, modally influenced recording "Kind of Blue," and his group included musicians such as Bill Evans and John Coltrane, who were already becoming major influences in their own rights. In every way a perfect example of Szwed's "high modernism," Davis was musically innovative in a modernist sense: modestly extending conventional norms, commercially successful, handsome, aloof and always fashionably dressed—an African-American "hipster" of the model given such exalted symbolic capital in Mailer's "The White Negro."[130] It may be no wonder, then, that Davis—who unlike Milt Jackson, had a considerable professional investment in being seen as the music's cutting edge—criticized Coleman so bitterly.

Any objections to Coleman's music that were in fact, "strictly musical" could possibly be related to A.B. Spellman's examples of jazz musicians who felt they must prove themselves "capable of playing classical music to show that playing the blues was a matter of choice."[131] The music of Coleman's quartet presented a similar challenge: to say that because one disliked it, one was unwilling to play it, carried the unspoken implication that one was unable to play it. As Coleman himself put it, his music challenged jazz musicians to question the practices they had worked so long and hard to master:

> When I arrived in New York... from most of the jazz musicians, all I got was a wall of hostility... I guess it's pretty shocking to hear someone like me come on the scene when they're already comfortable in Charlie Parker's language. They figure that now they may have to learn something else.[132]

Other musicians on Coleman's side echo this view. "When we played, there were those who really loved it, the growth and the spirit of it," said Don Cherry. "And then there were those who didn't like it because they felt it was jeopardizing their position in life."[133] Buell Neidlinger described the musicians at the Five Spot as "scared to death Ornette was going to be the thing and that they couldn't make it."[134] It is perhaps instructive that Neidlinger presents the problem as an imperative: if this music is "going to be *the* thing," then they are offered no alternatives. Similarly, Coleman asserted that having heard his music, "they may *have to* learn something else."

For its detractors, it was easy to turn their backs on Coleman, but demonstrating that they could master his idiom—in order to prove that ignoring him was a matter of choice—was not so easy. Despite the wide margins for error that were apparent in this new freedom, the Coleman group had a repertoire of pieces, to be played without reliance on chord changes, that they had thoroughly rehearsed. The leading names in jazz, generally skilled sight-readers thoroughly schooled in musical theory, and with enormous knowledge of conventional jazz performance practice, could learn the tunes, but the group's way of playing them was something unique and new.

Possibly this reveals something more about the intrinsic value of the symbolic capital possessed by each member of the jazz field. If a member could not countenance the procedures of the incoming avant garde, they were fortunate if, like Milt Jackson, they could move gracefully from an understated position in the modernist camp to the mainstream jazz canon which stood ready and willing to embrace and enshrine them.[135]

Not all jazz virtuosi were that lucky. Their inability to come to terms with Coleman's style meant that they effectively lost rank within the jazz field. The awful truth, as revealed in the acclaim bestowed on Coleman by the field's mediators, was that the positions of these musicians was no longer determined solely by the merit of their accomplishments—the extent to which, in the course of their careers, they had revealed new possibilities within the music they had been given. The paradigm of jazz performance had shifted, and it was made clear that an artist's future prospects would be judged on how much, or how little, it resembled that of the incoming avant garde, who had now been boosted to the peak of the field's hierarchy.

In other words: in terms of symbolic capital, if the most valuable currency within the field was possessed by those musicians seen as the most *au courant,* then after decades of working their way up through the hierarchy, the most respected artists in jazz were now clearly being sent back down. As Bley suggests in his remarks about the Jazztet, before Coleman's advent, the jazz virtuoso who had best mastered the song form occupied the field's most honoured position. Post-Coleman, it could be seen as a default position—the high modernist agenda now strongly suggested that musicians who continued to play within the song form did so only because they possessed insufficient artistic vision to grasp, much less embrace, the new style.

In these terms, it is possible that Coleman's fiercest detractors among the era's jazz musicians were reacting not to him or to his music, but to what they saw as a devaluing of their entire body of work and a threat to their status within the jazz field, a threat that menaced the integrity of the field as a whole. This threat came from both inside and outside the field.

Although many of the jazz musicians who objected the most strongly to Coleman's music eventually modified their positions, most historical accounts have recorded only those objections expressed on a strictly musical basis, and expressed in strictly musical language. There were another set of objections, raised by members of the jazz field who felt that Coleman was a pawn being manipulated by forces determined to dominate the field.[136]

THE MEDIATORS OF THE JAZZ FIELD

For all these mixed reactions, Paul Bley has said that jazz critics of the time:

> performed a yeoman service in quickly identifying Ornette's valid-
> ity to the skeptics... The critics did more than their job of
> acquainting the public with the music. They acquainted the *musi-
> cians* with the music. They acted as liaisons between the avant garde
> and the musical community.[137]

Bley differentiates clearly between the avant garde and the "musical community" at large, emphasizing the distance felt by jazz musicians between their music and Coleman's (if Coleman indeed began the "free jazz" revolution of the 1960s, he also began the still-ongoing problem of differentiating between "jazz" and "improvised music"). However, not everyone felt that the mediation of the critics was a good thing.

In a letter to *Down Beat* late in 1959, John Mehegan condemned the part that critics were playing in the public reception of the music:

> What [Coleman] is doing certainly has nothing to do with jazz and, I'm afraid, very little to do with music in any form... His reputation is completely the result of artificial promotion by a small group of king-makers... The frightening thing here is that a small group of writers can "launch" a young musician on a path that can only end in personal defeat and bitterness for the persons involved.[138]

Mehegan's letter is valuable less for its vehement objections to Coleman's music as for the precise placement of the author's non-musical objections in the laps of "a small group of king-makers." Even if Coleman's detractors could accept the sincerity of Coleman himself, they could not accept the exercise of power they saw in judgements of jazz critics, however well-intentioned might be the latter's "yeoman service."

Leonard Feather voiced similar reservations when, for 1960's first issue of *Down Beat*, he subjected Ornette Coleman to a Blindfold Test. In this regular *Down Beat* feature, a musician would be asked to identify and comment on recordings by unnamed jazz artists. Over the years the Blindfold Test served as an entertaining, if highly unscientific, litmus test of a musician's ability to recognize different artists and styles, a test which evoked unpredictable responses from jazz artists in all genres.

In Coleman's case, the allegedly rootless avant-gardist astutely identified most of the artists that he heard, and criticized their music precisely if idiosyncratically (Feather remarked that Coleman is "no less unusual in his verbal than in his musical expression"). But first, Feather prefaced the test with an introduction that took a firm critical stance on Coleman's notoriety, and in doing so echoed Mehegan in identifying the problem of power.

> In the early days, jazz talent took its natural course. Anybody with something new and important to say would find his way to the surface of public acceptance, simply on the strength of the stir he had created among fellow musicians.
>
> Today the situation is very different. The initiative in molding new stars has been seized by other experts, including some who were among the slowest to accord reluctant recognition to Dizzy Gillespie and Charlie Parker. Ornette Coleman, an alto saxophonist, who, until a few months ago, was virtually unknown, must suffer the judgements applied by the contemporary method.[139]

In the past, Feather is saying, established musicians were the first to acknowledge original new artists, by testing and tempering their abilities in the nightly workshop of the jazz engagement. Now, because the consensus of critics was supplanting this "natural" method, musicians might find themselves in the spotlight before their abilities had earned them a place there.

At the time he wrote this, Feather himself had been the USA's preeminent jazz critic for over twenty years. Since his arrival from England in the mid-1930s, his influence had been felt in the careers of countless American jazz musicians. Feather wrote reviews and books on jazz, and produced concerts and records. Although he also wrote songs that would occasionally be performed by jazz musicians, it was as a critic that he was principally known—a critic who did not hesitate to use his influence on behalf of music that he liked, or to denigrate or overlook music that he didn't like. So there is a disingenuousness in his complaint about the power of critics—presumably critics other than himself—to alter the "natural course" of jazz talent.[140]

Despite this, Feather's comments make a useful starting point for examining the workings of power within the jazz field. How in fact *did* Coleman—in person quiet and self-effacing—manage to make such a noisy, spectacular entrance into the jazz field? Was it in fact not just the power of his music, but the power of a "small group of king-makers" that engineered his leap into the spotlight?

In fact, some of the era's most influential and powerful individuals and institutions helped to boost Coleman into prominence. The chain of events that brought Ornette Coleman to the Five Spot combined the best efforts of critics, record producers, academics and the promotional forces of the music industry. It was a chain of events very different from the organic process that Feather champions as "natural," but one that plainly revealed the currents of power that are constantly at work within artistic fields. As Joe Goldberg wrote in 1965, recalling Coleman's first Five Spot engagement:

> Unfortunately, Coleman immediately became a scapegoat; critics used him as a shield behind which to take potshots at other critics. Two of Coleman's staunchest admirers were Nat Hentoff and Martin Williams, co-editors of *The Jazz Review*. The publisher of that magazine, Hsio Wen Shih, became Coleman's manager for a while. Some journalists began to see a Lenox–Atlantic–*Jazz Review* Establishment, forcing Coleman on the jazz world... With such poison pellets in the air, reasoned comment on Coleman's music became almost impossible.[141]

EIGHT
The Battle of the Five Spot

I think if there had been some secret way they could have all just had Ornette disappear, an atomizer you know—go downtown and put a guy's name on a card and drop it into this machine and push the button and it would atomize him—he would have been out in space years ago. Lots of cats would have put his name in that machine and done that (laughter).

— trumpeter/composer Bobby Bradford, 1976[142]

Pierre Bourdieu depicts the artistic field as a fiercely politicized society. As in any society, struggles for survival and struggles for power—in other words, struggles to maintain one's current position, or improve it, even at someone else's expense—are waged continually. Although in day-to-day interactions, members acknowledge each other as equals, in reality the field has a rigid hierarchy. It is a pyramid that only has room for a select few at its apex.

Competition is fierce. All members must confront the challenge of aspiring to a higher position within the field, while holding on to such status as they already possess. Taste, as we have seen already, is one of the markers with which each individual stakes out his or her area of personal distinction.

However, membership in the field has its own rewards regardless of position. If it is not altogether a self-contained universe, it is at least a community, a social village with a finite membership. Within its boundaries, all members have the satisfaction of knowing their place, of having an identity, of having other members know their names. So to be a member of an artistic field is in itself already a certain kind of success, but most members—membership itself having fired their ambitions—are goaded to seek ever increasing success.[143]

Gunther Schuller wrote in 1997, for a reissue of Coleman's 1960 recording *Free Jazz:*

Hearing this music nearly 40 years later, much of the shock effect has worn off. Free playing is no longer the novelty it once was. There is hardly a jazz musician worth talking about in the last two generations—the postbop era—who, whether as a soloist or as part of a collective ensemble, has not at some time and in some way improvised freely, eschewing basic harmonic progressions, themes, and motives, as well as the standard song or tune repertory.[144]

In the same vein, Frank Tirro has written:"The strength of the reaction, in retrospect, is somewhat amusing, for Coleman's music, by the standards of the classical avant-garde musicians of the day, was neither new nor shocking."[145]

This may be true if we approach the music from a strictly positivist viewpoint, reviewing it simply in terms of its techniques. Coleman broke out of jazz's traditional structures, but instead of more imposing or more sophisticated structures, he offered the alternative of improvisational freedom. In a period when the future of jazz was seen in more fully composed works for larger ensembles, his "harmolodic" group improvisations de-emphasized the role of the composer and re-emphasized the primacy of collaboration among a small group of peers. At a time when jazz was beginning to be taught in academies heretofore dedicated to European music, and increasingly was interpreted as an "art" music, the raw timbre and relaxed tonality of his quartet evoked the country blues sound of Coleman's Texas heritage, and for many listeners reaffirmed jazz as a folk music, and an essentially African-American one at that.

Certainly what Trevor Tolley wrote years later about Archie Shepp (in 1959, an up-and-coming young avant-gardist who was to draw great inspiration from Coleman) can equally be said about Coleman himself:

As time passes, the great innovators of jazz appear as the makers of the jazz tradition. Their roots in that tradition appear stronger and stronger, until it requires an effort of the imagination to see how they in fact revolutionized the music.[146]

Why then, one must ask, could no one at the time offer Coleman the assured place in the jazz canon that we extend to him today?

Of course, the jazz field *was* the field within which the music was received—not that of the classical avant garde,[147] essentially a concert music strongly oriented toward the classical canon and its attendant infrastructure: the conservatory, the university and the concert hall. In contrast, jazz in 1959 was still played mostly in bars. Among its audience, even the most dedicated aesthetes were expected to move about the room and socialize while the music was playing, and above all to subsidize the event by buying drinks. It would take another fifteen years for the phenomenon of the multi-disciplinary gallery/concert venue—such as New York's The Kitchen or The Knitting Factory—to confront the issue of programming both avant-garde jazz and classical music on an equal basis, presenting along with these different musics the assumption that they shared an aesthetic kinship—that although they might approach musical problems differently, they were on equal terms as elite art forms.

Meanwhile Coleman's music was being judged by the prevailing standards of all the members of the field, both supporters and detractors, who treated the issues around it with utter seriousness.[148]

CONSECRATION/LEGITIMATION

Acceptance means *legitimacy*. To be accepted within an artistic field, one's art must be deemed legitimate either by consensus or by the approval of the most powerful members of that field. Bourdieu refers to this process of legitimization as *consecration*.[149]

With these terms in mind, we can begin to see why Coleman in 1959 was so controversial. He did not appear—was not allowed to appear—at the Five Spot as a blank slate on which anyone might inscribe their own interpretation. By the time he took the stage on his first night, powerful consecrating forces were already working on his behalf. In many cases it was these forces to which his critics, and even his audience reacted, as much as to the music itself.

On one occasion, according to A.B. Spellman, the USA's leading classical composer and conductor of the time, Leonard Bernstein, sat in on piano with Coleman's group.[150] If this in itself wasn't enough to align Bernstein with the incoming avant garde, one night the composer, like Mailer at Taylor's engagement a few years before, went out of his way to make sure that all those present knew his position. He "... leaped to his feet at the end of one set and declared that 'this is the greatest thing that has ever happened in jazz' and that 'Bird was nothing.'"[151] Although a persuasive consecration from a man who was, at the time, probably the most prominent and respected figure in American music, such a display must have only caused further resentment among jazz musicians who, in effect, were being told that their tastes, aesthetics and hard-earned abilities were now obsolete.[152]

CONSECRATION BY PEERS

When you come to New York there are certain customs and protocols. It's a tradition that for the first twelve months you're seen and not heard. You attend all the events, you make friends, but essentially it's considered gauche to expect anyone to hire you just because you're the hot flash from out-of-town, so you do a great deal of listening.[153]

Paul Bley is describing the first stages of what John Szwed has called "the jazz recruitment process."[154] In John Litweiler's words, it was:

Part of the orthodox bop attitude of the day... the belief that only musicians who had worked as sidemen for established New-York-based leaders for a period—paying their dues, the practice was called—deserved success.[155]

Coleman of course had never satisfied the demands of this New York protocol: he had never played with or even auditioned for Miles Davis, Dizzy Gillespie, Horace Silver, Art Blakey or any of the other New-York-based jazz leaders. In fact, he had never before been to New York. He had never allowed himself to be judged, mentored, employed or fired by any of the established jazz artists who now crowded the Five Spot to hear him. If he had done so with any degree of success, he could have gained an entry level position as a "sideman" within the jazz field's musical hierarchy. This was traditionally a first step towards becoming a "leader."

If then, in an alternative course of events, Coleman *had* fulfilled these protocols, how would his music have fared? We might look at a Coleman contemporary, Cecil Taylor, as a model for speculation.[156]

Taylor was a native New Yorker and, from the time the Termini brothers took over the club, an occasional performer at the Five Spot. His percussive, densely clustered piano style presented a challenge to standard jazz performance practice that was as radical as anything that Coleman had to offer.

However, Taylor possessed legitimizing qualifications—in other words, jazz credentials—that Coleman did not have. After extensive early training, and four years at the New England Conservatory, Taylor had gained entry to the jazz field through observing the unwritten protocols that Bley describes. Years of avid listening in New York clubs were followed by apprenticeships with swing musicians Hot Lips Page, Johnny Hodges and Lawrence Brown. Taylor then began leading his own groups, and developing his style in an increasingly free, non-tonal direction. His music was not popular with the majority of musicians in the jazz field, but his background and observation of the field's protocols enabled him to be recognized as a legitimate member.

In Taylor's case, recognition did not necessarily mean success. In a field dominated by bebop virtuosos such as Dizzy Gillespie, Sonny Rollins and Max Roach, the understated "cool" jazz of Gerry Mulligan, Chet Baker, Miles Davis, and the Modern Jazz Quartet, and the blues revival of Horace Silver, Art Blakey and Cannonball Adderley, Taylor's aggressive, atonal style was an anomaly. By the time Coleman arrived in New York, despite the loyal support of a few critics such as Nat Hentoff, Taylor had made few recordings, was chronically under-employed (even by the desperate standards of most musicians trying to make a living playing jazz), and had found a few colleagues who were willing and able to play his music.

By observing the protocols, Taylor had been admitted to the field by the consensus of established members. However, that consensus also kept him in a marginalized position that would be no threat to the position of any other member—where, although his music may have gained him some grudging respect, it looked unlikely that it would ever gain the exposure needed to make it "the shape of jazz to come."[157]

Coleman, on the other hand, made his first New York appearance as a leader. He debuted in a club made prestigious by its association with uncompromising musicians such as Taylor, Randy Weston, Charles Mingus and Thelonious Monk, leading a band of equally untried and non-"recruited" (or "unconsecrated") sidemen. Arriving by this unique route, Coleman bypassed the "customs and protocols" that would have allowed the members of the jazz field to judge him, admit him, and once having admitted him, to marginalize him, as Taylor had been marginalized.[158]

Aided by the economic capital of a major record company and the symbolic capital granted by influential critics and other mediators, Coleman impacted like a meteor on the jazz field. These consecrating forces rammed him into a prominent position that forced the field's established members to defend, to redefine and even to relinquish the positions they had worked long and hard to gain. Although the shock of his entry was personally out of character for the polite, soft-spoken Coleman, his comment on the stresses of established jazz musicians who "now… may have to learn something else" revealed that he was alert to the implications of his arrival.

In reality, of course, rather than "learning something else," an older generation of musicians would have to cope with being displaced in position and forced to move downward through the field hierarchy. In effect, it seems possible that the actual sound of Coleman's music was made more shocking by what was interpreted as the colossal rudeness, the elbowing-aside of established protocols, even the bullying, with which it arrived. To call it, in Goldberg's words, "a Lenox–Atlantic–*Jazz Review* Establishment" (in fact instead of "establishment," perhaps "conspiracy" was closer to what he meant) was not necessarily far off the mark.

CONSECRATING FIGURES

Contemporary Records first recorded Ornette Coleman in 1958 with a group including bassist Don Payne, who played a test pressing of the session for Nat Hentoff and John Tynan, the West Coast correspondent for *Down Beat* magazine. Tynan reviewed the record enthusiastically in *Down Beat* and tried unsuccessfully to convince the prestigious Monterey Jazz Festival to present Coleman.[159]

Meanwhile, partly through Payne's continuing advocacy, Coleman came to the attention of two members of one of the era's most respected jazz groups, the Modern Jazz Quartet. After Coleman and Cherry persuaded the MJQ's bassist, Percy Heath, to play on their second Contemporary record, the group's pianist, John Lewis, took an interest in the music and soon had convinced the MJQ's label, Atlantic, to record them.

Although Coleman's fame was launched by a series of advocates working separately and together, simultaneously and consecutively, John Lewis was possibly the central consecrating figure in the process. A talented, conservatory-educated composer and arranger, and a pianist who worked with Dizzy Gillespie, Charlie Parker, Miles Davis and Lester Young in the 1940s, in 1951 he and Milt Jackson founded the Modern Jazz Quartet. Throughout the 1950s the MJQ, with their subdued sound and their tuxedos and with Lewis as musical director, actively strove to promote their music as high art, and to perform whenever possible in concert venues rather than clubs. Lewis himself was instrumental in pioneering Third Stream performances and the concept of jazz education, co-founding the summer Lenox School of Jazz in Massachusetts in 1957.[160]

The Modern Jazz Quartet's mellow piano-vibraphone-bass-drums sound was disparaged by some members of the jazz field as too mild and conciliatory (in fact, too bourgeois), and their adoption of classical forms as a denial of African-American heritage. However, as a black group making a success of themselves in the music industry, playing essentially a concert music, they were important pioneers. Robert Walser has written:

African-American performers and composers have long worked to defeat racist essentialism by proving their ability to write and perform European concert music. The chamber jazz of the Modern Jazz Quartet, with its cool fusions of swing and classical forms, was also a statement of black pride, however conservative it seemed amid the turmoil of the 1960s.[161]

Whatever the jazz field's reservations about the MJQ's music, no one denied the high level of their musicianship. With their commercial and critical success, and his own compositions for ballet, theatre and film, by the late 1950s Lewis was a ground-breaking educator, a respected artist, an influential figure and a powerful consecrating force.

In the spring of 1959 he turned the full force of his influence to Coleman's benefit. Atlantic Records was a large independent company with a diverse catalogue and wide distribution that made an Atlantic contract an enviable goal for a musician—a goal that many well-established jazz artists could not achieve.[162] Atlantic's promotional aggressiveness made itself clear as soon as it took on Coleman as one of its artists. The Contemporary records had been titled "Something Else!" and "Tomorrow Is the Question"—titles that alerted the listener to something new and innovative. The first Atlantic record was called "The Shape of Jazz to Come," soon followed by "Change of the Century." The more insistent titles left no room for doubt: Coleman's music, Atlantic announced, was The Next Big Thing, with which all jazz listeners, and players, would have to contend, whether they liked it or not.

Meanwhile, as artistic advisor to the Monterey Jazz Festival, Lewis was able to book Coleman into the 1959 festival—a prestigious, high-profile venue that only a year before had turned down a similar initiative from John Tynan.[163] As director of the Lenox School of Jazz, Lewis arranged for Coleman and Cherry to get scholarships (paid for by Atlantic) to the summer 1959 sessions—less for the program's curricular benefits than to introduce the men and their music to the musicians and writers on the Lenox faculty.[164]

At Lenox, Gunther Schuller and *New York Times* jazz critic Martin Williams were both impressed with Coleman. Both praised him privately and in print, and their influence opened further doors. Williams was instrumental in convincing the Termini brothers to book Coleman's group into the Five Spot, and in the months to follow, Schuller wrote music featuring Coleman as soloist, and gave him private theory lessons.[165]

But for all their good works on Coleman's behalf, Lewis can still be seen as the major consecrating force. Unlike most of the prominent musicians in the New York jazz field, Schuller was an academic, and a white academic at that; to some black members of the field, he would always have a degree of outsider status. Williams was a white critic who wrote about a black music form; his reputation would vary among the field's members, probably in proportion to how fairly each of them felt his or her work had been treated.

In contrast, Lewis's status in the field was unassailable. In his youth, he had honoured the unwritten protocols of working for the field's most prominent leaders, and had duly advanced through the ranks to leading his own group. The Modern Jazz Quartet had carved a distinctive niche for itself in the international music world: on one hand it boasted Lewis's sophisticated compositions and arrangements and on the other Milt Jackson, the leading jazz vibraphonist of his generation, along with the superb instrumental talents of Percy Heath and drummer Connie Kay. As a black composer, artistic advisor and educator, Lewis had made significant inroads into areas traditionally dominated by whites. The endorsement and support of a figure as widely respected as Lewis was an essential consecration; a consecration that the field's other members could dispute, but which none of them could ignore.

NINE: CONCLUSION
The Jazz Field

Throughout this book, references to "the jazz field" might allow for two different definitions. In recalling the Ornette Coleman controversy, I have treated the milieu of his first Five Spot performances as a microcosm of that field.

The "jazz field" in question might include everyone in the world who is actively involved with the music—a record collector in Cairo, a guitar player in Beijing and a club owner in Milan—regardless of location, nationality or ethnicity. Or, the "jazz field" may be read as synonymous with "the New York jazz field," weighting the term with the tacit assumption that the era's major players were all based in New York City, as were most of the major critics, scholars and record companies.

One of these definitions situates the jazz field within the boundaries of New York City. The other envisions the jazz field as a community literally without borders of nation and geography. In fact both of these views of the jazz field are accurate, and both co-existed actively in the jazz music of 1959, even as they do today.

An artistic field is an economic as well as a social and artistic entity, and all major cities, with their performance venues, art galleries, schools, publishers and studios, tend to attract artists and to become regional artistic centres. This is especially true in music. Depending so much on the abilities of their fellow group members for the success of each night's performance, musicians, even moreso than other artists, gravitate to centres where the best players, and in a pinch their substitutes, are immediately available. It is even more true for jazz musicians, since it is even harder to find players who can not only read and interpret scores, but be interesting and original improvisers.

Throughout the twentieth century, New York City was the undisputed world capital of jazz music, the centre to which all jazz musicians of the top rank must eventually gravitate.[166] To best advance not only their music, but their reputations, musicians came to New York, and throughout jazz history it has been the base for tours, recordings and criticism, and the site for the creation of careers and eventually of canons. Because of this, acceptance in the New York jazz field has become the ultimate test of a musician's legitimacy. There is no better proof of the latter statement than the career of Ornette Coleman.

WEST COAST JAZZ

The origins of jazz as a music that came up the river from "New Orleans, the traditional birthplace of jazz"[167] are increasingly disputed, as historians discover accounts of similar musical movements developing contemporaneously across the continent. However, what has not changed in accounts of jazz history is the depiction of the music's ultimate destination as New York and New York only, undervaluing its vital developments in—to cite the USA alone—Chicago, Kansas City and points west.

For example, Ted Gioia has pointed out that early New Orleans musicians such as Jelly Roll Morton, Kid Ory and King Oliver lived and worked in Los Angeles and San Francisco before 1920. He even traces the earliest use of the term "jazz" itself to a San Francisco bandleader in 1914.[168] However, as well as championing the US west coast as a site of musical ferment, Gioia challenges the ways of disseminating and documenting jazz music that restrict the creation of canonic figures and movements to New York, and points out that the eastern bias has affected jazz reputations from the music's earliest days:

> Jelly Roll Morton, in words that could be written today, remarked about a trombonist from Oakland from the pre-Prohibition years: "Poor Padio, he's dead now, never got East so none of the critics ever heard him."[169]
>
> Outside of a few individuals such as Les Koenig and Richard Bock, the west largely lacked the non-musical resources—the behind-the-scenes support groups made up of journalists, impresarios, and the like—that are often crucial in determining what gets heard and what gets neglected. In the short run, such outside figures often hold the key to a musician's commercial viability; in the long run, they affect nothing less than how the history of the music is written.[170]

Gioia's history of the California jazz scene enables the reader to form an impression of the course that Ornette Coleman's career might have taken if he had stayed there, and not been swept up so suddenly into New York's jazz circles. For westerners such as Coleman and Charles Mingus, moving their music to New York eventually gained them opportunities to collaborate, perform and record in a cultural centre where they would be heard, discussed and written about, and where they could much more readily form relationships with musical peers as well as with the gatekeepers of the music industry, not only in New York but in the nurturing European scene, now a mere ocean away. The move to New York won them positions as canonic figures and enabled their music to become a major influence. But for musicians who stayed in California such as Buddy Collette, Teddy Edwards, Hampton Hawes and many others, decades of accomplishment still left their contributions marginalized as "West Coast Jazz."

As we have seen, throughout the 1950s, despite making little headway with bebop players, Coleman had found musical collaborators and managed to perform occasionally. His first recordings for the Los Angeles label Contemporary had garnered him only modest attention. It is reasonable to surmise that had he stayed in Los Angeles he, like so many other west coast musicians, could have built a substantial body of work and still remained no more than a footnote in official jazz histories.

Similarly, had Coleman brought his saxophone and his sheet music to New York, acting only on his own initiative, one can imagine he would have been greeted with the same mixed, predominantly negative reactions he had received in Los Angeles. Like Cecil Taylor before him, he could have worked his way into the jazz field, but probably only on the same marginalized level accorded Taylor. If Coleman had brought his whole band to New York unannounced, unsponsored by consecrating figures or institutions, it would certainly have been a brave but short-lived experiment. It seems doubtful that they would have found enough work to support themselves. Would a high-profile club such as the Five Spot have been interested?

Instead however, Coleman appeared in New York already heralded (although the words were never his) as a heroic figure, in the words of A.B. Spellman, "a walking myth, the image of a small bearded man striding out of the woods of Texas and into New York's usually closed jazz scene."[171] Due to the consecrating efforts of John Lewis, Gunther Schuller, Atlantic Records and a host of enthusiastic and proactive critics, Coleman immediately became famous, not only as a musician but as a divisive and controversial figure.

When Pierre Bourdieu wrote, "nothing more clearly affirms one's 'class,' nothing more infallibly classifies, than tastes in music," he made possible a study such as this one, which tries to show how on this occasion struggles for power worked their influence within the jazz field, all the while expressing themselves in the language of musical taste. In the Coleman dispute, such expressions of taste marked each individual's allocation of cultural capital, hence each one's status within the field.[172]

Once Bourdieu's ideas have been placed in this context, a universe of possibilities becomes apparent. How do his notions of taste, field and the three artistic positions apply to the widely diversified musics that constitute "jazz" today? How did they work throughout the careers of major figures such as Louis Armstrong, Billie Holiday, and Charlie Parker? How do positions within the field differ for black and white artists, for men and for women?

It would be fascinating, for example, to look at the jazz field around Duke Ellington's performance at the 1956 Newport Jazz Festival, when an extended version of *Diminuendo and Crescendo in Blue* revived Ellington's career as a popular "bourgeois" artist in a time that he was in danger of being consigned to the museum of "art for art's sake."

Similarly, the late 1930s saw ground-breaking concerts by Benny Goodman (Carnegie Hall, New York 1938) and Marian Anderson (Lincoln Memorial, Washington D.C. 1939) that could be seen as redefinitions of their respective fields. Goodman's brought jazz music, and black performers, to the stage of a major classical concert venue,[173] and Anderson's affirmed—in fact, insisted—that black performers could qualify fully as members of the classical field.[174]

ONCE AGAIN, THE LATEST THING

Since the 1980s, Wynton Marsalis, a New York-based trumpeter and composer who has also become a powerful mediator in the jazz field, has loudly asserted a definition of jazz that confines the music to the strict forms and steady rhythms that Coleman so readily transgressed. In effect, Marsalis champions a field *without* an avant garde, although this has always been the way for established, and conservative, members of artistic fields: to draw a line, and deny membership to those who cross it.

However, with the huge support this position has recruited, both from performing arts institutions and the music industry, and the benefits it has bestowed on established jazz musicians working in the song form, it is hard to foresee the appearance of a consecrating figure who might possess enough will and enough power to boost musical innovators over this line.

Perhaps the new recidivism will work, and jazz will become, like classical music, essentially a repertory art where new members will gain admittance according to how well they interpret the existing canon. Genuine innovators will have to find a niche elsewhere, or create their own and as always, rely on the curiosity of interested listeners to seek them out.

But where does this leave the high modernist agenda—the search for the revolutionary sound, the new genius? For now, the agenda has been co-opted by Marsalis and the new conservatism. The movement that began a quarter-century ago, with Columbia's search for a replacement for the "hipster" trope that Miles Davis was violating, with his embrace of pop music's flashy costumes, electric instruments and back-beat, resulted in an ingenious strategy. After all, as Gendron points out, the discursive binaries of traditionalism and modernism pivot around a disdain for the status quo, a disdain that is shared equally by both sides.

Columbia reasoned that it should be possible to create a new star, a "hipster" in the high modernist image, a rebel who turns his back on prevailing musical trends—but who, in doing so, does not go forwards into the unknown, but backwards into well-trodden territory. By promoting such an image, Columbia, and the other industry members that followed it, could not only recapture an older jazz audience, but convince a younger generation of musical consumers that the familiar tropes identified with jazz—the aloof hipster with the horn, the elder statesman hunched and focused at the piano, the *chanteuse* with her strapless evening gown—were once again, the latest thing.

TWO WORLDS OF JAZZ

Eric Hobsbawm has pointed out that Coleman came to New York at what was possibly the peak moment of twentieth-century jazz: "At no time before or after was it possible to enjoy the entire range of music live, from the survivors of the 1920s to the anarchist sonorities of Ornette Coleman and Don Cherry… with some notable exceptions the great names on which my generation had been raised were still in operational form."[175]

This remained more or less true throughout the 1960s. Despite the fact that the tsunami of rock music, as it buoyed popular music to new heights of success, pushed jazz even farther into the margins of the industry, the jazz canon seemed to be gradually growing. After the shock of Coleman's style, John Coltrane's steps from the song form to thunderous free improvisations, overtly part of the artist's personal spiritual quest, made him one of the few jazz artists embraced by the counterculture surge of the 1960s. Albert Ayler's music, although less marketable than Coltrane's, shared some of the same appeal, and the styles of both of these saxophonist/composers suggested a new kind of jazz, one in which free improvisation could act as a unifying force between traditional and new song structures, between music from cultures around the world, and even between players of very different levels of ability.

This promise began to be fulfilled during the 1970s, but not by Coltrane, who died in 1967, or Ayler, who died in 1970. Beginning in that decade, the music began to lose its seminal figures: Louis Armstrong in 1971, Duke Ellington in 1974, Charles Mingus in 1979. To jazz devotees, each of these deaths felt like the end of an era, but the decade also brought forward a number of new candidates for the jazz canon, among them Anthony Braxton, Leo Smith, Roscoe Mitchell, George Lewis, Julius Hemphill, Anthony Davis and Oliver Lake. But only in rare cases did their music fit well into the gradually evaporating club circuit. Intense, exploratory, its forms often as severe and demanding as its improvisations, their music and the extent to which they applied their creativity to other forms (through-composed pieces, electronic music, performance art), won its own generation of listeners, but nothing approaching the mass audience that the industry was looking for in its own quest to perpetuate the canon. With Miles Davis semi-retired and in ill health, Columbia Records, trying to recapture the appeal of a hipster with a horn playing standards, signed tenor saxophonist Dexter Gordon, and looked for a new trumpet star to replace Davis. They tried Freddie Hubbard, then Woody Shaw, and finally settled on a young trumpeter playing with Art Blakey, Wynton Marsalis.

By this time, both the Art Ensemble of Chicago and Cecil Taylor had become stars in their own right, not through major-label promotion (as in the case of Coleman and, to strike an uneasy parallel, Marsalis) but through a long progress from smaller to larger concert venues and independent record labels.

The AEC and Taylor, in fact, were prime examples of artists who, despite the influence they exerted, remained in the jazz field's avant garde. Despite the acclaim of critics and, at times, their ability to draw large audiences, their respective musical languages were never adopted as standard practice by the jazz mainstream.

In effect, by this time the musicians and supporters had moved into two separate fields which, although they may overlap in their esteem for pre-Coleman jazz, tended to position themselves very differently in regard to that body of work.

For the sake of convenience one might classify these two fields as "mainstream" and "free" jazz. In this case, "mainstream" indicates an orientation around song forms—an example of a contemporary "mainstream" jazz musician could be tenor saxophonist Joe Lovano, regardless of the liberties he may pursue within those forms. "Free" essentially stands for post-Ornette-Coleman jazz, including such musicians as alto saxophonist Anthony Braxton and bassist Barry Guy, and referring not to any insistence on total improvisation—many of these musicians are active composers—but to the breadth of sounds and the span of references that these artists perceive as permissible within the genre.

EPILOGUE

The language of Bourdieu, as is that of much cultural theory, is a cold hard economic language. Yet Bourdieu's writings stand out for the warmth, humour, and love of humanity embedded within their dense language and their unique perspectives on society and its structures. If his theories of societal "fields" might seem too deterministic for some, others may find them liberating in their matter-of-fact revelations that even in the arts and academia—notorious staging areas for the nurture and display of asocial or anti-social tendencies—each of us thinks and acts as a social creature, down to the last molecule.

Although I have been involved with jazz and improvised music on many levels for many years (from completely improvised cello performances, to playing string bass in dance bands at small-town Legion halls, from editing *Coda* jazz reviews as I typeset them, to writing academic papers in graduate school), I am still capable of waxing sentimental about the music. The music itself is all about feeling, but sentiment is often about loading feelings with more existential weight than they merit. To offset this tendency, cultural theory can be an effective tool for the reassessment of music, the other arts and their place in this vast web of interactions and exchanges we call society.

Over the years, as a member of several overlapping jazz fields (Toronto / Canada / North America / world), I have partaken fully in the structure of "positions and position-takings." Seeing it in the light of Bourdieu's theories has been a welcome revelation. I loathe musical snobbery—even my own, which is considerable—and I looking forward to further reading and deeper understanding of Bourdieu's work, all the better to arm my own anti-snobbery arsenal.

These are fruitful areas for inquiry and discovery, especially insofar as they might prompt the reader to examine and reexamine his or her own position. After all, whether as researcher, listener, scholar, critic, producer, publisher, player or composer, we are all contributing members of the jazz field.

AFTER THE FIVE SPOT

This book discusses Ornette Coleman's music roughly from 1958 to 1960 which was, of course, only the beginning of Coleman's recording career, and by no means defined this artist's ever-evolving style.

In the mid-1960s, Coleman emerged from a period of retirement playing trumpet and violin as well as saxophone. In the 1970s, he formed the group Prime Time and made his first recordings with electric guitar and bass. The 1980s brought Shirley Clarke's film "Ornette: Made in America," and a successful collaboration with the popular jazz guitarist Pat Metheny. During these years, fans who yearned for the original acoustic quartet could listen to Old and New Dreams, a quartet formed by Coleman's erstwhile collaborators Dewey Redman, Don Cherry, Charlie Haden and Edward Blackwell, that played original compositions as well as Coleman's.

Coleman began the 1990s working with Howard Shore on the soundtrack to David Cronenberg's film adaptation of the William Burroughs novel *Naked Lunch*. Later in the decade, he returned to the acoustic format in his working groups, adding pianist Geri Allen. During all these years, Coleman has continued to produce through-composed works for a variety of ensembles. At the end of 2005, he was touring with a quartet consisting of his son Denardo on drums and two acoustic bassists.

ORNETTE COLEMAN QUARTET: MASSEY HALL, TORONTO, OCTOBER 29, 2005[176]

Jazz in a jazz club is a night out, jazz at Massey Hall is a bit of a pilgrimage. For more than half a century the place has been sacred ground, ever since the May 1953 concert there by Charlie Parker, Dizzy Gillespie, Bud Powell, Charles Mingus and Max Roach began circulating on record, hyped as "the greatest jazz concert ever." Legendary as it soon became, that event was sparsely attended—a problem not suffered by Ornette Coleman in 2005 as hundreds of people crowd the floor and rim the balconies of a space that, in an age when the clubs are struggling but stadium concerts sell out, seems cozy and nostalgic.

Coleman is of course a pivotal figure, the last avant-gardist to make it into the jazz canon before the Marsalis/Crouch neo-cons bricked up the entrance. His music appeared at the end of the 1950s as the segue between jazz's traditional song forms and much wider horizons of sound—a transition that by no means did everyone want to make. Coleman's music itself was seen as angry and divisive, when in reality it was, and is, generous and inclusive.

At Massey Hall he took the stage with his son Denardo Coleman on drums and two acoustic double bassists, Tony Falanga and Greg Cohen. Once the quartet began to play, the sheet music in front of them became incidental to the music's near-telepathic interplay. For the most part, Cohen played pizzicato, his fluid rhythmic partnering with Denardo offering a multi-textural embrace to Falanga's arco obbligati and Coleman's plaintive, vocalized alto saxophone. A brief passage with the leader on violin moved the ensemble into territory that Coleman, Cecil Taylor and Albert Ayler pioneered in the sixties, a keening, atonal string timbre that had never been heard in jazz before and that became a major influence on many of the next generation's improvisers.

Whether executed at a fast or slow tempo, there was an elegiac feeling to everything that Coleman played in this concert. At age seventy-five, perhaps his attack is not quite so vigorous as it was twenty or forty years ago, or his technique quite as sharp—but his concept is as clear as ever. By and large, there is a sharp division in jazz between those who play wonderfully and those who play perfectly, and Coleman's alto saxophone has always been firmly on the "wonderful" side.

Despite Coleman's legendary status, I never expected to see such a large crowd at a mainstream venue like Massey Hall for what is, after all, free jazz. How did they like it? After an hour-and-a-quarter the music ended, the ensemble left the stage, and the crowd rose in a standing ovation. The quartet came back and played as an encore Coleman's best-loved composition, *Lonely Woman*.

As a listener I applauded and as a musician and, I suppose, a jazz scholar, I felt grateful for the chance to hear Coleman playing his own music in its full acoustic glory. If as a musician he has shown other musicians how to be freed from structural constraints, as an artist his example has given artists in all disciplines the permission to free themselves. His theory of "harmolodics" cannot be understood in strictly musical terms because it is so much a theory of relationships, and a model of how humans can work together mutually, uncompromisingly, lovingly, to create something dynamic and beautiful. It is a model that has helped many of us to understand and to cherish not only the music that came after Ornette Coleman, but the music that came before him.

In the context of music in 2005, his son's lustrous drumming, the organic timbres of the two acoustic basses, and the cry of Coleman's saxophone sound project a warmth that renders irrelevant any questions of tonality or atonality, tradition, modernism or postmodernism. Above all, where others play "the blues" as a scale and a set of changes, Coleman has sustained the blues cry, that lonely sound that makes us feel that for a moment we are not alone.

As for upsetting any notion of Massey Hall as a jazz mecca—I can't help you there. I went to hear a living legend—thinking that after all this time Coleman owes us nothing and has nothing to prove—and came away exhilarated from hearing great music. As far as I'm concerned, this creaky old concert hall is still sacred ground.

ACKNOWLEDGEMENTS

This book is an adaptation of the master's thesis I wrote for the MA program in Music Criticism offered by the School of the Arts (SOTA) at McMaster University, Hamilton, Ontario, Canada. Even before writing the thesis, however, I had dealt with this subject in several different forms.

I entered the program in September 2002, and the following spring, Roseanne Kydd's encouragement and comments helped me through my first attempt to write about Ornette Coleman, jazz critics and the Five Spot. Ajay Heble prompted me to further develop the topic for the colloquium of the September 2003 Guelph Jazz Festival. Later that fall, having been introduced during my studies to some of the writings of Pierre Bourdieu, I was able to begin applying Bourdieu's ideas to Coleman's Five Spot debut in a colloquium that Sandy Thorburn presented on musical topics at SOTA.

It was Susan Fast who, responding to my first curious email back in 2002, phoned me at my home in Pender Harbour, answered all my questions and facilitated my application and acceptance. Dr. Fast supervised my first attempts at roughing out a thesis in my reading course (including a complete change of topic a month in), coached me through SOTA's acceptance of the new topic for my master's thesis and turned me over to James Deaville as advisor. As head of the Music Criticism program during my first year at McMaster, Susan was able to skillfully and sympathetically ensure that my abilities and the program's mandate worked to each other's advantage.

I was lucky to have Jim Deaville as thesis advisor as well as instructor in two graduate courses. In my second year at McMaster, during the Christmas break, he threw me a curve in suggesting that I lay aside a perfectly good thesis topic (*Jazz and the Image of Romantic Genius*) in which I had invested many hours, in favour of expanding a term paper on Ornette Coleman into my MA thesis. My desk still surrounded by stacks of books on Coleman, Pierre Bourdieu, and modern jazz, I readily took up his challenge and Jim was a great help in helping me see it through. Each time I delivered a new draft or chapter, he got back to me promptly with notes and comments that were always positive, humorous and insightful.

I must thank my other instructors who were so vital to making the MA program in Music Criticism such a positive experience: Mary Cyr, William Renwick, and especially Paul Rapoport, whose "Practical Music Criticism" sessions helped me make the difficult transition from the workaday world into academic life. All of my fellow grad students had much more formal musical background than I do, and all of them were willing and eager to shore up my weak spots on the many occasions when it was necessary: Annemarie Camilleri, Jane Clifton, Kate Davies, Tina Depko, Nick Donlevy, Deborah Henry, Rebekah Jordan, Shona Moiny, Dan Sheridan, Tim Smith and Jennifer Taylor.

Finally among my academic affiliations I should acknowledge the second and third readers of my thesis: Christina Baade, especially for steering me towards writings that were essential to my arguments about the evolution of jazz criticism, and Hugh Hartwell, whose knowledge of jazz I depended on to help keep me on track in my descriptions of the music's history and the Five Spot milieu.

Outside of McMaster, I am grateful to Canada's foremost jazz scholar, Mark Miller, for bringing to my attention the Olin Downes review referred to on page 106 and supplying me with a copy. Graham Taylor's "nit-picking and pedantry" (his description not mine) actually represented considerable reading, time and thought on his part; he called my bluff on a number of significant matters, and I only regret that, with deadlines looming, I've not been able to do justice to all the points he was considerate and learned enough to raise. Beverley Daurio has been not only daring enough to take this on as a publishing project, but insightful and meticulous in her editing. In a more general sense I must thank John Norris and Bill Smith, who in 1975 hired me to work at the Jazz & Blues Centre in Toronto, opening up for me a daily exposure to the music and musicians that lasted for eight years.

For all this, it was a comment made many years ago by pianist Paul Bley that led me to investigate the role played by critics in Ornette Coleman's rise to prominence. Working with Bley on his autobiography, I was impressed with the truth of his perspective of the workshop nature of life on the bandstand—that the practice of jazz is itself a university where deep analysis, risk-taking and intense motivation bring the greatest rewards.

For all of the above expertise I have been able to call upon, and all the references I have been able to muster, writing a work of this length consists largely of sitting at a keyboard and putting down one's own ideas, with all their possible idiosyncrasies and misinterpretations. Among other things, although Ornette Coleman has been part of my musical life for thirty years, my introduction to Pierre Bourdieu is still very recent, and the application of his ideas to jazz is still very much a work in progress. For any factual errors or sins of omission that may have found their way into this book, I can only take full responsibility.

David Lee

SOURCES

Adderley, Julian. "Cannonball Looks at Ornette Coleman." *Down Beat* 27.11 (26 May 1960).

Ake, David. "Re-Masculating Jazz: Ornette Coleman, 'Lonely Woman', and the New York Jazz Scene in the Late 1950s." *American Music* 16.1 (Spring 1998).

Allen, R.E. *The Pocket Oxford Dictionary of Current English*. Seventh edition. Oxford: Clarendon, 1984.

Anderson, Marian. *My Lord, What a Morning*. New York: Viking, 1956.

Bailey, Derek. *Improvisation: its nature and practice in music*. Ashbourne, UK: Moorland, 1980.

Baldwin, James. *The Price of the Ticket: Collected Nonfiction, 1948–1985*. New York: St. Martin's/Marek, 1985.

Balliett, Whitney. *Collected Works: A Journal of Jazz 1954–2000*. New York: St. Martin's, 2000.

Baraka, Amiri, see Jones, LeRoi.

Bley, Paul, with David Lee. *Stopping Time: Paul Bley and the Transformation of Jazz*. Montreal: Véhicule, 1999.

Bourdieu, Pierre. *Distinction: A Social Critique of the Judgement of Taste*. Trans. by Richard Nice. Cambridge, MA: Harvard UP, 1984.

——. *The Field of Cultural Production: Essays on Art and Literature*. Ed. Randal Johnson. New York: Columbia UP, 1993.

——. *Meditations pascaliennes*. Paris: Collection Liber/du Seuil, 1977.

Burton, Humphrey. *Leonard Bernstein*. New York: Doubleday, 1994.

Carr, Ian, with Digby Fairweather and Brian Priestley. *Jazz: The Essential Companion*. London: Grafton, 1987.

Cerulli, Dom, Burt Korall, and Mort Nasatir, eds. *The Jazz Word*. London: Dobson, 1962.

Chambers, Jack. *Milestones II: The Music and Times of Miles Davis Since 1960*. Toronto: Toronto UP, 1985.

Coleman, Ornette. Liner notes. "Beauty Is a Rare Thing." *This Is Our Music*. Atlantic SD 1353; CD reissue Sepia Tone 02, 2002. Recorded 2 Aug. 1960.

Dance, Stanley. "Lightly and Politely." *Jazz Journal* 13.2 (Feb. 1960).

Davis, Miles, with Quincy Troupe. *Miles: The Autobiography of Miles Davis*. New York: Simon & Shuster, 1989.

DeMicheal, Don, and Ralph Gleason. "In Review." *Down Beat* 24 Dec. 1959.

DeVeaux, Scott. *The Birth of Bebop: A Social and Musical History*. Berkeley: California UP, 1997.

Edmiston, Susan and Linda D. Cirino. *Literary New York: A History and Guide*. Boston: Houghton Mifflin, 1976.

Feather, Leonard. *The Encyclopedia of Jazz*. New York: Bonanza, 1960.

Gendron, Bernard. "'Moldy Figs' and Modernists." Gabbard, Krin, ed. *Jazz among the Discourses*. Durham, N.C.: Duke UP, 1995.

Gillespie, Dizzy, with Al Fraser. *To Be or Not To Bop.* Garden City, NY: Doubleday, 1979.

Gioia, Ted. *West Coast Jazz: Modern Jazz in California 1945–1960.* New York: Oxford UP, 1992.

Goldberg, Joe. *Jazz Masters of the Fifties.* New York: Macmillan, 1965.

Gourse, Leslie. *Straight, No Chaser: The Life and Genius of Thelonious Monk.* New York: Schirmer, 1997.

Gridley, Mark. *Jazz Styles: History and Analysis,* fourth edition. Englewood Cliffs, NJ: Prentice Hall, 1991.

Haden, Charlie. E-mail correspondence with the author, May 4, 2006.

Heble, Ajay. *Landing on the Wrong Note: Jazz, Dissonance, and Critical Practice.* New York: Routledge, 2000.

Hentoff, Nat. *The Jazz Life.* London: P. Davies, 1962. Reprinted. New York: Da Capo, 1975.

Hobsbawm, Eric. E-mail correspondence with the author. 18 May 2005.

——. *Interesting Times: A Twentieth-Century Life.* London: Abacus, 2002.

——. *The Jazz Scene.* New York: Pantheon, 1993.

Hoefer, George. "Caught in the Act." *Down Beat* 7 Jan. 1960.

Honneth, Axel, with Hermann Kocyba and Bernd Schwibs. "The Struggle for Symbolic Order: An Interview with Pierre Bourdieu." *Theory, Culture & Society* 3.3 (1986): 35–51.

Huyssen, Andreas. *After the Great Divide: Modernism, Mass Culture, Postmodernism.* Bloomington: Indiana UP, 1986.

Jones, LeRoi (Amiri Baraka). *Black Music.* New York: Apollo, William Morrow, 1968.

——. *Blues People: Negro Music in White America.* London: The Jazz Book Club, MacGibbon & Kee, 1966.

Kotlowitz, Robert. "Monk Talk." *Harper's* Sept. 1961.

Lane, Jeremy F. *Pierre Bourdieu: A Critical Introduction.* London/Sterling, VA: Pluto, 2000.

Litweiler, John. *Ornette Coleman: A Harmolodic Life.* New York: William Morrow, 1992.

Lott, Eric. *Love and Theft: Blackface Minstrelsy and the American Working Class.* New York: Oxford UP, 1993.

Mailer, Norman. *Advertisements for Myself.* London: Andre Deutsch, 1961.

McDarrah, Fred W. *Beat Generation: Glory Days in Greenwich Village.* New York: Schirmer, 1996.

McMichael, Robert K. "'We Insist—Freedom Now!': Black Moral Authority, Jazz, and the Changeable Shape of Whiteness." *American Music* 16.4 (Winter 1998).

Miller, Mark. *Some Hustling This! Taking Jazz to the World 1914–1929.* Toronto: Mercury, 2005.

Miller, Terry. *Greenwich Village and How It Got That Way.* New York: Crown, 1990.

Mills, Hilary. *Mailer: A Biography.* New York: Empire, 1982.

Mingus, Charles. *Beneath the Underdog.* New York: Penguin, 1971.

Monson, Ingrid. "The Problem with White Hipness: Race, Gender, and Cultural Conceptions in Jazz Historical Discourse." *Journal of the American Musicological Society* XLVIII.3 (Fall 1995).

Olson, Lynne. *Freedom's Daughters: The Unsung Heroines of the Civil Rights Movement from 1830 to 1970.* New York: Scribner, 2001.

Panish, Jon. *The Color of Jazz: Race and Representation in Postwar American Culture.* Jackson: Mississippi UP, 1997.

Peyser, Joan. *Bernstein: A Biography.* New York: Beech Tree, William Morrow, 1987.

Ploski, Harry A., and Warren Marr, II, eds. *The Negro Almanac: A Reference Work on the Afro American.* New York: Bellwether, 1976.

Podhoretz, Norman. *Making It.* London: Jonathan Cape, 1968.

Priestley, Brian. *Mingus: A Critical Biography.* London: Quartet, 1982.

Ramsey Jr., Guthrie P., *Race Music: Black Cultures from Bebop to Hip-Hop.* Berkeley: California UP, 2003.

Rivers, Larry, with Arnold Weinstein. *What Did I Do? The Unauthorized Autobiography.* New York: HarperCollins, 1992.

Rollyson, Carl. *The Lives of Norman Mailer: A Biography.* New York: Paragon, 1991.

Russell, George, and Martin Williams. "Ornette Coleman and Tonality." *The Jazz Review* 3.3 (June 1960).

Sadie, Stanley, ed. *The New Grove Dictionary of Music and Musicians,* second edition. London: Macmillan, 2001.

Schuller, Gunther. *Musings.* New York: Oxford UP, 1986.

——. Booklet accompanying CD reissue of *Free Jazz: A Collective Improvisation by the Ornette Coleman Double Quartet.* Santa Monica, CA: Rhino, 1998.

Shapiro, Nat, and Nat Hentoff. *The Jazz Makers.* New York: Rinehart, 1957.

Simosko, Vladimir, and Barry Tepperman. *Eric Dolphy: A Musical Biography & Discography.* New York: Da Capo, 1979.

Smith, Bill. "The Paul Bley Interview: A Conversation with Bill Smith." *Coda* 166 (April 1979).

Spellman, A.B. *Black Music: Four Lives* (originally *Four Lives in the Bebop Business,* 1966). New York: Schocken, 1970.

Szwed, John. *So What: The Life of Miles Davis.* New York: Simon & Shuster, 2002.

Tirro, Frank. *Jazz: A History,* second edition. New York: Norton, 1993.

Tolley, Trevor. "Archie Shepp, CW'S, Ottawa, April 10, 1980." *Coda* 173 (1980).

Walser, Robert. *Keeping Time: Readings in Jazz History.* New York: Oxford UP, 1999.

——. *Running With the Devil: Power, Gender, and Madness in Heavy Metal Music.* Hanover, NH: Wesleyan UP, 1993.

Ward, Geoffrey C. *Jazz: A History of America's Music.* New York: Knopf, 2000.

Weber, Mark. "Bobby Bradford Interview." *Coda* 157 (Sept.-Oct. 1977).

Wilmer, Valerie. *As Serious as Your Life: The Story of the New Jazz.* Westport, CT: Lawrence Hill, 1980.

Wilson, John S. "Jazz at Town Hall." *The New York Times* 21 Nov. 1959.

RECOMMENDED INTERNET SOURCES

On the internet, more complete discographic information can be found at http://www.jazzdisco.org/ornette/dis/c/, as well as Robert Stubenrauch's discography at http://www.geocities.com/BourbonStreet/Quarter/7055/ Ornette/Disco-ornette.htm. A greater variety of information, including an essay on references to the Five Spot engagements in Thomas Pynchon's novel *V.*, is offered by musician and critic David Wild at http://home.att.net/~daw-ild/ornette_coleman.htm. For the most up-to-date information, Ornette Coleman himself has a home page: http://harmolodic.com.

NOTES TO THE TEXT

Introduction: The Field of the Five Spot (pages 11-13)

1. Gourse, 130–132.

2. Rivers with Weinstein, 341-2. Painter/saxophonist Larry Rivers (1923–2002) takes credit for initiating informal jam sessions at the Five Spot, or at least for encouraging Joe Termini, who apparently did the booking, to look beyond these sessions and make jazz part of the club's business. Rivers identifies the white bebop saxophonist Allen Eager as the first jazz artist to perform there.

3. Spellman, 10–11.

4. Litweiler, 78.

5. Spellman, 9. Spellman's interview with Joe Termini circa 1966 reveals the club owner to be not so sympathetic to jazz as to put the music's needs above his own: "I might not have jazz in the future. People seem to like dancing, and I might go into that... If I lose money, I won't have jazz anymore." On page 8 of the same article, Cecil Taylor's bassist Buell Neidlinger relates how the Terminis consistently tried to curtail the length of the group's sets, so that the audience would start ordering drinks.

6. Ibid, 6–7.

7. Chambers, 19, lists these names among the audience. The poet/photographer Fred W. McDarrah, in *Beat Generation: Glory Days in Greenwich Village* (New York: Schirmer Books, 1996), p. 103, recalls taking Jack Kerouac late in the evening on December 10, 1959 to hear Coleman at the Five Spot, where "the place was nearly empty except for [painters] Franz Kline and William Morris."

8. Edmiston and Cirino, 124–141.

9. Frank O'Hara, "The Day Lady Died," *The New American Poetry,* Donald M. Allen, ed., (New York, Grove Press, 1960).

10. Edmiston and Cirino, 138.

11. Miller, cited in Panish, 27.

1. The Arrival of Ornette Coleman (pages 14-18)

12. Ward, 417. A photograph shows a lineup in the street outside the Five Spot during Coleman's November 1959 debut.

13. Ibid.

14. Ibid, p. 75.

2. Jazz and Ornette Coleman (pages 19-25)

15. Leonard Feather, *The Encyclopedia of Jazz* (New York: Bonanza Books, 1960), 23. In addition to the inherent thoroughness of its research, the publication date of this venerable reference work makes it especially valuable in recapturing the ambience of the

jazz field at the time of Coleman's emergence. For example, one of its appendices (p. 479) includes a special sub-section on "Reactions to (and by) Ornette Coleman."

16. Spellman, 5, brings this perspective: "The black musicians, such as John Lewis and J.J. Johnson, who were involved in what has been called Third Stream music... belong to a tradition in jazz in which one first proves oneself capable of playing classical music to show that playing the blues was a matter of choice. This tradition goes back to Jelly Roll Morton, James P. Johnson, and Willie 'The Lion' Smith, who once boasted that he could 'play Chopin faster than any man alive.'"

17. Gridley, 55. The ODJB's historic 78 rpm record had *Livery Stable Blues* on one side and *Dixie Jazz Band One-Step* on the other. As a commercial hit that exerted a huge musical influence, this 78 is liable to maintain its status as "the first jazz record" for the foreseeable future. However Mark Miller, 28–29, nominates the 1916 recordings made in England by the African-American group The Versatile Four as earlier and possibly more authentic contenders.

18. Feather, 23. At this time of writing (2006), virtually all serious scholars agree that jazz originated with black Americans, but in fact this is exactly what Feather disputes in his historical overview. A lifelong champion of black American music, he was also a champion of white contributions (including by implication his own, as pianist and songwriter) to the jazz idiom. Although his overview confirms the facts of early jazz that I list here, like other presumably well-intentioned writers of his generation (for example Marshall Stearns in *The Story of Jazz,* 1956), Feather chooses not to acknowledge the imbalance of power between white and black musicians within the music industry as a factor in the music's history. Instead, he celebrates the steady accession to popularity through which jazz styles gradually became accepted by larger audiences. In such a narrative, white popularizers such as the Original Dixieland Jazz Band, Paul Whiteman and Benny Goodman come across as benevolent, paternalistic figures "paving the way" (one of Feather's favourite terms) for the music's black originators.

19. Ibid, 371.

20. Ibid, 24–25, 460.

21. Ibid, 27.

22. Feather, 155 (Carter entry) and 250–251 (Henderson).

23. Carr et al., Henderson entry by Digby Fairweather, 227.

24. There are few major artists whose position in the jazz canon takes such roller-coaster soars and dips as does that of Brubeck (1920–). On one hand he is demeaned for his music's popularity and accessibility, and for his admittedly unsubtle piano technique; on the other hand he is lauded for his original compositions, his experiments with odd time signatures and for his personal warmth and charisma. Black avant-gardists such as Anthony Braxton and Cecil Taylor have praised him as an early inspiration—Braxton even recorded with Brubeck in the 1970s—although as Taylor has said, "I found Brubeck's work interesting until I heard [Art] Tatum, Horace Silver, and Oscar Peterson..." Spellman, 62.

25. Walser, ed. *Keeping Time,* 9–11, is the source here for composer/conductor Ernest Ansermet's famous review, "Sur un Orchestre Nègre" (*Revue Romande,* Switzerland 1919). Until the discovery of Downes' 1918 Clef Club Orchestra review in the *Boston Sunday Post* (see following note), Ansermet's piece was often cited as the first time that jazz was eulogized as high art by a white "consecrating figure" from the classical music world. Ansermet praises the music of James Reese Europe's orchestra, applying the term "genius" both to the ensemble's music and to the work of its leading soloist, clarinet Sidney Bechet.

26. Olin Downes, *Boston Sunday Post*, August 4, 1918. In this review, predating Ansermet's by a year, Downes praises the black musicians of the Clef Club Orchestra, and concludes that "The musical art of the Negro should be welcomed, encouraged, and cultivated in this country for the great and significant thing which it is, and not merely as the passing amusement of an idle summer's evening."

27. Jones (Amiri Baraka), *Blues People*, 216–220.

28. Schuller, in Cerulli et al., 185.

29. Ibid, 184.

3. Ornette Coleman in Los Angeles (pages 26-33)

30. Litweiler, 25.

31. Schuller, in Sadie, ed., 99.

32. Schuller, *Musings*, 27–28.

34. Ibid, 29.

35. Ibid, 21–44.

36. Litweiler, 57 and 147. Although Coleman refers to *Lonely Woman* (c. 1959) as the first "harmolodic" composition he recorded, he did not use the term publicly until 1972.

37. Ian Carr et al., 216.

38. Litweiler, 46–48, suggests that strictly musical objections might have made up a fairly minor component of Coleman's rejection by established musicians. He presents evidence that the saxophonist's appearance and demeanor, and even the type of instrument that he played, were also important factors. Coleman had long hair and a beard, both indicators of nonconformity (especially for an African-American) that would certainly brand him as an outsider in the Los Angeles jazz scene of the time. Regardless of how the music sounded, a working jazz musician might not want to share his stage with a figure whose very appearance could offend paying customers. In addition, Coleman played an inexpensive plastic alto saxophone, an instrument many musicians did not take seriously. And his low-key demeanor and quiet, high-pitched voice worked against him in a conservative social milieu, marking him as a possible homosexual (which was occasionally presumed), or at any rate as an eccentric who could be easily denigrated or bullied. However, by the time he began making records in 1958, Coleman had cut his hair and shaved off his beard, and photos from the time present him in tidy sweaters and slacks.

39. Ibid, 50–55.

40. Paul Bley with Lee, 24.

41. Ibid, 25–26.

42. Russell, Cerulli et al., 190-192.

43. Bley with Lee, 61.

44. Ibid, 63.

45. Russell and Williams, 9.

4. Beauty Is a Rare Thing (pages 34–35)

46. Coleman, liner notes, 1960, identifies the concert C played by the trumpet as a D. As has often been noted, first by his latter-day teacher Gunther Schuller, the transposing of different instrumental parts (always the source of discussion, and even confusion, in any ensemble) was a skill that the largely self-taught Coleman had not quite perfected, and is thought to have contributed to his distinctly edgy harmonic sense both as player and composer.

47. Ibid.

48. Litweiler, 88.

5. Pierre Bourdieu and the Concept of "Field" (pages 36–45)

49. Lane, 9.

50. Spellman, 83.

51. Litweiler, 23–4. Coleman sums up his background by saying, "I didn't come from a poor family, I came from a *po'* family. Poorer than poor."

52. Lane, 9. The citation given is an interview with Bourdieu by Honneth et al., 1986. Nowhere in the interview does Bourdieu sum up quite as neatly as this his conversion from philosopher to sociologist, nor in such a precise time frame. However his statements throughout the interview—for example, that in the late 1950s, "I saw myself as a philosopher and it took some time until I realized that I had become an ethnologist." (38), taken together, confirm the accuracy of Lane's summary.

53. Tirro, 376. "… the introduction of any of these concepts [atonality, compositional indeterminacy] into jazz had never been accomplished with any security before the thirty-year-old Coleman took his stand... The miracle worth noting, however, was the speed with which this music influenced jazz and engendered a major style change."

54. Bourdieu, *Meditations pascaliennes*, 77. Quoted in Lane, 3.

55. Lane, 3.

56. I may be guilty here of stereotyping the French intellectual in the Parisian bistro, à la *Round Midnight* and other films that depict French bohemia, but I am also thinking of the long-standing advocacy of jazz by so many in the French intelligentsia: the seminal critics Hughes Panassié and Andre Hodeir, the multi-disciplinary artist Jean Cocteau, filmmakers such as Louis Malle and Roger Vadim who commissioned soundtracks from American jazz musicians, etc.

57. Bourdieu, *Distinction*, 16.

58. Bourdieu, *The Field of Cultural Production*, 5.

59. Ibid, 4–5.

60. Bourdieu, *Distinction*, 5–6.

61. Allen, 770.

62. Bourdieu, *Distinction*, 18–19.

63. Ibid, 16.

64. Bourdieu, *The Field of Cultural Production*, Randal Johnson, "Editor's Introduction," 7.

65. Bourdieu, *Distinction*, 2.

66. Bourdieu, *The Field of Cultural Production*, Randal Johnson, "Editor's Introduction," 7–8.

67. Bourdieu, *The Field of Cultural Production*, 161–175.

68. Ibid, 162.

69. Ibid, 162–164.

70. Ibid, 34.

71. Ibid, 166.

72. Ibid, 167.

73. Ibid, 60.

74. Ibid, 121.

75. McMichael, fn. 413.

6. The Culture of the Jazz Club (pages 46-58)

76. Mingus, 249–250, cited in McMichael, 392.

77. McMichael, 393.

78. Baldwin, 289; originally published in *Esquire*, May 1961.

79. Podhoretz, 110. This particular artistic field is vividly described as a "family" by Podhoretz in this memoir. As a young man, Podhoretz was eager to join the New York literary "family" of the 1950s. He justifies the term *family* "by the fact that these were people who by virtue of their tastes, ideas, and general concerns found themselves stuck with one another against the rest of the world whether they liked it or not (and most did not), preoccupied with one another to the point of obsession, and intense in their attachments and hostilities as only a family is capable of being." Podhoretz takes pains to point out that the interests and activities of family members continually crossed genre boundaries; it was an "intellectual" family rather than a strictly literary one. His "family's" relationships of power and position match Bourdieu's account of field relationships; so does his account of their genre-crossing predilections, as exemplified by the presence of Baldwin and Mailer, two members of the literary "family" whose names also appear in accounts of the Five Spot.

80. Spellman, 11.

81. Mills, 207. Since Coleman's quartet played again at the Five Spot from April through July 1960, this return engagement was the probable occasion for Mailer and Felker's "spring of 1960" meeting.

82. Ibid, 206–207.

83. Mailer, "The White Negro: Superficial Reflections on the Hipster," *Advertisements for Myself* 284–5.

84. Monson, 398.

85. Ibid, 415.

86. Rollyson, 110, describes that around the time that Mailer was writing "The White Negro," "he rented a saxophone in order to 'honk' along with the music of Thelonious Monk. Although he could not play the instrument, Mailer believed he was in tune with it, that he was 'hip.'"

87. Monson, 420.

88. Panish, "Racing the Village People: Euro American and African American Cultural and Social Interaction in Greenwich Village, 1945–1966," *The Color of Jazz*, 26.

89. Ibid, 26–27. Baldwin had to remove himself from his cultural background in order to join the intellectual field represented at the Five Spot. This, in fact, was true to some extent of most of the field's members. Again, Norman Podhoretz provides a graphic description of the necessity of severing one's ethnic roots (in his case, working-class Brooklyn Jewish) in order to join the "family" (or field) of intellectual Manhattan, when he describes his reaction to the uplifting intentions of "Mrs. K.," a high school teacher who took him under her wing and exposed him to high culture: "And how could she have explained to me that there was no socially neutral ground to be found in the United States of America, and that a distaste for the surroundings in which I was bred, and ultimately (God forgive me) even for many of the people I loved, and so a new taste for other kinds of people—how could she have explained that all this was inexorably entailed in the logic of a taste for the poetry of Keats and the painting of Cézanne and the music of Mozart?"

90. Baldwin, 320–323.

91. Litweiler, 91.

92. Gioia, 351. Although this anecdote agrees with other stories of Coleman's reception at the time, Mel Lewis might have had his dates mixed up, since other accounts have John Lewis encountering Coleman's music no earlier than 1958, and Schuller not until he heard him at Lenox in 1959.

93. Bley with Lee, 63.

94. Ibid, 68. "The owner of the Hillcrest… was in denial. This band had done so well for him. Three of its original members were still on the bandstand… It took him a month to realize that he could no longer afford having an atom bomb go off in his club every night. With much regret, he told us that he had to let us go."

95. Hobsbawm, (writing as Francis Newton) in *New Statesman*, reprinted in *The Jazz Scene*, 271. A typographical error prevented the author from researching its references properly but Dr. Hobsbawm was kind enough to clarify one point via e-mail: "Butlins (not Butins) was a famous and popular holiday camp company. Filey was one of its more popular locations on the English east coast. You can imagine what kind of music that sort of place enjoyed. The reference would have been easily understandable in Britain when I wrote my article in 1960 but I can see that it is now very obscure."

96. Ibid.

97. Balliett, 82–83.

98. Ibid, 192.

99. Cerulli et al., 71. Bob Rolontz, "What Became of Jazz and Poetry?", *The Jazz Review*, New York (Feb. 1958).

100. Kotlowitz, 21–22.

101. Advertisement, Argo Records, *The Jazz Review*, June 1960, inside front cover.

102. Dance, 23.

103. Paul Bley, from interviews with the author, unpublished, 1985–88. Guy Lombardo led a popular "sweet" dance band, playing sentimental favourites, for so many decades that his name was often used as a synonym for banal, old-fashioned dance music.

7. The Musicians and the Critics (pages 59-74)

104. Bourdieu, *The Field of Cultural Production*, 35–6.

105. Gendron, 32.

106. Ibid, 50.

107. Ibid.

108. Ibid.

109. Szwed, 107.

110. Andreas Huyssen, *After the Great Divide: Modernism, Mass Culture, Postmodernism* (Bloomington: Indiana University Press, 1986). "…an increasingly consuming and engulfing mass culture," p. vii. Quoted in DeVeaux, 443.

111. Bourdieu, *The Field of Cultural Production*, 40.

112. Wilson, 26.

113. Litweiler, 55. Coleman recalls Dolphy having been "cold" to him in his Los Angeles period, although in New York they became friends and recorded the album *Free Jazz* together. On p. 46, on the other hand, Litweiler quotes Dolphy recalling that he had heard Coleman in 1954 and praised his music.

114. Simosko and Tepperman, 36.

115. "In Review." *Down Beat*, Dec. 24, 1959, 39–40.

116. Hoefer, 40–41.

117. Lott, 51, quoted in Monson, 405.

118. Monson, 412.

119. "A&R" stands for "artists and repertoire." The era's common term, "A&R man" has for many years now been supplanted by the term "record producer."

120. Hoefer, 40.

121. Shapiro and Hentoff, xi. This collection of essays on jazz artists identifies contributor Hoefer as having "conducted the 'Hot Box' column in *Down Beat* for more than 20 years and has written for *Esquire, Metronome, Tempo,* and other jazz publications."

122. Among his many crusading actions on behalf of the music, Hentoff published and co-edited his own jazz magazine, *The Jazz Review,* from 1958 to 1961 and in the same period started a record company, Candid.

123. Hentoff, 228–9.

124. Goldberg, 231.

125. Bourdieu, *The Field of Cultural Production*, 53.

126. Chambers, 20.

127. Litweiler, 83.

128. Priestley, photo signature between pp. 148 & 149, includes William Claxton's photograph of "Newport 'rebels' Mingus and Roach with Kenny Dorham and Ornette Coleman; Cliff Walk Manor Hotel, 3 July 1960."

129. Shelly Manne, *2-3-4,* Impulse! Records Stereo A-20, 1962.

130. Szwed, 148–9. In fact, Davis and Mailer knew each other well and even engaged in romantic rivalry over actress Beverly Bentley, who eventually married Mailer. It has been suggested that Mailer's "hipster" was largely modeled on his perception (shared by many others) of Davis, an image that, admittedly, was encouraged by the trumpeter himself.

131. Spellman, 5.

132. Hentoff, 231.

133. Wilmer, 69.

134. Hentoff, 231.

135. The innovations of John Lewis' compositions and arrangements were always subtle and pleasing to the ear. This, combined with subdued timbre of the ensemble's sound and the tuxedoed gentility of their stage image, made the MJQ a very unthreatening avant garde—and at the same time, one whose professionalism was never questioned.

136. Musicians often softened their objections towards Coleman once they met him and realized his own stance on their music. Anecdotes reveal that at the end of his Five Spot sets opposite the Farmer/Golson group, Coleman always announced the upcoming "great music" of the Jazztet. Julian "Cannonball" Adderley wrote, "When introduced to Ornette, I received praise and admiration to the point of embarrassment." Adderley also described trombonist/composer Bob Brookmeyer as hating Coleman & Cherry's music when he heard it at Lenox, but coming to accept it during the Five Spot engagement. (Adderley, 21). Canadian jazz musician Dave McMurdo adds to this the anecdote, related to him by Brookmeyer, that the trombonist's attitude towards Coleman broadened even more in the early 1960s, when he recognized Coleman as a loyal repeat customer at club engagements of the Brookmeyer/Clark Terry quartet.

137. Smith, 4.

138. *Down Beat*, Dec. 10, 1959, 6.

139. *Down Beat*, Jan. 7, 1960, 39–40.

140. Gourse, 38. Behind Feather's comments in the *Down Beat* test is an implicit disapproval of Coleman's music that was characteristic of this critic's reception of postswing jazz styles. Fifteen years earlier, Feather had been literally strong-armed into writing more favourably about the emerging styles which came to be known under the name of "bebop," including the music of the distinctive pianist/composer Thelonious Monk. As Monk's son related the story: "Feather had previously written very critical articles about Thelonious. Monk was extremely upset. One day the big, intense pianist grabbed Feather, a slender, almost reedy-looking man, by the collar—or the 'neck,' as one person recalled it—and threatened to throw him over a guard wall at Rockefeller Center. There was a big drop to the ground below on a level that was a popular, sunken ice-skating rink. 'You're taking the bread out of my mouth!' Monk said." It is perhaps no coincidence that soon after this incident, Feather's attitude softened toward the music of Monk and his contemporaries, culminating in his 1950 book, *Inside Bebop*. Although Feather never became a champion of Monk and his music, he at least withdrew his opposition to the field's acceptance of Monk as an important innovator: a rare instance of a member of an artistic field physically coercing the consecration of an influential mediator.

141. Goldberg, 235.

8: The Battle of the Five Spot (pages 75-83)

142. Mark Weber, "Bobby Bradford Interview," *Coda*, Issue 157, Sept./Oct. 1977, 5.

143. Baldwin, 320–323. Perhaps Baldwin identified the structure of the nightclub itself as a "field" when he described its habitués "peeping at each other in order to find out [if]…they are really having fun," and the "invisible barriers… which must not be crossed."

144. Schuller, booklet accompanying CD reissue of *Free Jazz*, 5.

145. Tirro, 376.

146. Tolley, 32.

147. To begin with, there were no black instrumentalists/ composers such as Coleman and Don Cherry in classical avant-garde circles of the time. That there are any now— mostly to the extent that "new music" concert series and festivals will now admit some avant-garde "jazz" into their programming—is due to the gradual progress Coleman, George Russell, Cecil Taylor and others made in gaining entry to those circles in the 1960s. At the same time in Europe, musicians such as John Stevens, Alexander von Schlippenbach, Misha Mengelberg, Willem Breuker and Gunter Hampel were exploring similar frontiers (von Schlippenbach's Globe Unity Orchestra even served as a catalyst for a collaboration between Don Cherry and Polish symphonic composer Krzysztof Penderecki in 1971). Experiments with new compositional forms and extended instrumental techniques were expanded upon in the 1960s and afterwards by such musicians as the Chicago AACM school (Anthony Braxton, Roscoe Mitchell, Leo Smith et al.) and the British improvising community that included Derek Bailey, Evan Parker, Barry Guy, etc.

148. Although Litweiler offers, between expressions of loathing from Max Roach and English critic Stanley Dance, examples of Coleman-inspired humour such as the joke, repeated to him by Coleman himself, about the couple hearing a nightclub waiter drop a tray of dishes: "'Listen dear, Ornette's playing our favorite song!' *Down Beat* columnist George Crater, who claimed to have invented an Ornette Coleman windup doll—wind it up, and it forgets the chord changes'—raised the question of whether an evening spent listening to Ornette was covered by Blue Cross." Litweiler, 83.

149. Bourdieu, *The Field of Cultural Production*, 50–51.

150. Spellman, 128. However, in response to a query about a passage in the Larry Rivers autobiography (342) in which Rivers describes Bernstein sitting in on bass at the Five Spot (a startling claim, considering that Bernstein was never known to have studied bass) Charlie Haden replied, "I can verify that Leonard Bernstein did not at any time play my bass. But I can confirm that he came into the Five Spot very often. Larry Rivers probably saw him on the stage, but what he was seeing was Leonard Bernstein on the stage putting his ear as close to my bass as he could to hear the notes I was playing. He did this on the first night he heard the band. He at no time played my bass, nor did he perform with the band." Haden, May 4, 2006.

151. Chambers, 19–20. "Bird" was of course alto saxophonist and composer Charlie Parker (1920–1955), who in style and technique was perhaps the strongest prevailing influence on the jazz musicians—indeed the entire jazz "field"—of the 1950s.

152. Hentoff, *The Jazz Life*, 232. Bernstein also invited Coleman to hear Dave Brubeck perform his brother Howard's *Dialogues for Jazz Combo and Orchestra* with the New York Philharmonic. "Coleman was bored by the music, and was stunned by the

scenes of homage in the Green Room where Bernstein receives visitors after the concert." This was apparently the end of their association. It is a tribute to Bernstein's power as a consecrating figure that, although few if any overviews of Coleman's career neglect to mention Bernstein's endorsement, this author has scanned through a library shelf full of books by and about Bernstein without finding even a passing reference to Coleman.

153. Bley with Lee, 36.

154. Szwed, 236. The full quote reads, "The other menacing music, free jazz, then still called the 'new thing,' sounded as if it had zoomed in from outer space, played by musicians who often seemed to have completely escaped the jazz recruitment process. They were classically trained virtuosos and musical illiterates, intellectuals and street rebels, and highbrows disguised as primitives."

155. Litweiler, 80.

156. Spellman, 5.

157. Spellman, 13–14, articulates the jazz field's problem coping with Taylor: "It was not the same reaction that Ornette Coleman received from musicians and critics, who said that he did not know how to play his instrument. Cecil obviously knew how to do that. It was that Cecil's music was an abrupt challenge to the hard bop music with its ready availability to both performer and listener. Unless Cecil would just go away, music would never be the same, and the musical scene would never be the same."

158. Carr et al., 487. The issue of marginalization versus canonization is critical. In fact, some observers have seen the Coleman controversy as detrimental to Taylor's career, deflecting attention from the pianist just as he was consolidating his style. Ian Carr's entry on Cecil Taylor includes this revealing sentence: "The whole jazz scene in the late 1950s was ripe for a shake-up, which happened with the advent of free jazz, and Taylor should have played a very prominent role as one of the trail-blazers of abstraction; but the arrival in New York of Ornette Coleman, in the autumn of 1959, put Taylor completely in the shade, blighting his career for several years." The late saxophonist Steve Lacy, in Bailey, 72–73, says, "There was complete opposition to what [Taylor] was doing in the '50s. To me in New York he was the most important figure in the earlier '50s. Then when Ornette hit town, that was the blow."

159. Litweiler, 60–61.

160. Carr et al., 298–299.

161. Walser, *Running With the Devil*, 61.

162. Litweiler, 66.

163. Ibid, 70.

164. Ibid, 68.

165. Ibid, 70.

9. Conclusion: The Jazz Field (pages 84–91)

166. Davis with Troupe, 86. An example of New York's symbolic importance is Davis' terse description of how he and his New York-based peers assessed Charles Mingus's bass playing when they first heard him in Los Angeles in the 1940s: "We... knew that he would have to come to New York, which he did."

167. Tirro, 6.

168. Gioia, 61.

169. Ibid, 62.

170. Ibid, 358–9.

171. Spellman, 79.

172. Bourdieu, *Distinction*, 18–19.

173. Carr, et al., 195.

174. Anderson, 184–196.

175. Hobsbawm, *Interesting Times*, 394–5.

After the Five Spot (pages 93-96)

176. This review originally appeared in a slightly different form as "Ornette Coleman: Onstage in a Jazz Mecca," *Coda*, Issue 325, Jan./Feb. 2006, 10.

INDEX

ABOUT THE AUTHOR

David Lee was born and raised in Mission, BC. Upon finishing English studies at UBC, he moved to Toronto where he worked for the jazz magazine *Coda* and with his wife, Maureen Cochrane, ran the publishing house Nightwood Editions.

He also studied double bass and became active in Toronto avant-garde theatre, dance and multi-media performances, as well as touring internationally and recording with the Bill Smith Ensemble. Lee's instrumental work can be heard on reissued Boxholder CDs with Leo Smith ("Rastafari") and Joe McPhee ("Visitation"), and on a recent Static Airport Records CD with Kenny Baldwin ("Row Boat to China").

Moving back to the west coast, he played in community bands, co-founded the Pender Harbour Jazz Festival, wrote a Vancouver Island guidebook, and co-authored *Stopping Time,* the autobiography of jazz pianist Paul Bley. David Lee received his MA in Music Criticism from McMaster University in 2004 and currently lives with his family in Hamilton, Ontario.